REAL MEN

WORSHIP WOMEN

A Gentleman's Guide to Loving & Obeying Women

Marisa Rudder

Please contact: Marisa Rudder

Email: femaleledrelationshipbook@gmail.com

Printed in the United States of America

Publisher's Cataloging-in-Publication data

ISBN # 978-09991804-2-6

Dedication

I would like to dedicate this book to all the strong, brave ladies who have joined or about to join the Love & Obey movement and live a female led lifestyle. Men must try to please their women at all times. All men must learn to serve women sincerely because of their love and respect for them. It is also my desire that every male will experience the joy of being a gentleman and the nobility of chivalry by entering into a loving Female Led Relationship (FLR). Each male will be exposed to a state of sexual and emotional ecstasy, which is created by loving, obeying and serving a devoted female authority figure. If you have not already, please join us ladies and gentlemen on social media. You can find out more at our website:

www.loveandobey.com

FACEBOOK
https://www.facebook.com/femaleledrelationships

TWITTER
https://twitter.com/loveandobeybook

YOUTUBE -
https://www.youtube.com/channel/UCkX3wmd934WR103hStbzbiQ

INSTAGRAM
https://www.instagram.com/femaleledrelationships

FOREWORD

WARNING: This book contains controversial female led lifestyle ideas and practices. So, please be careful what you ask for in life because you just might get it. Be advised that once you open the door to a female led lifestyle, there is usually no turning back. Once you've chosen your woman to be your Queen, she will demand a total 100 percent obedience from you. For some men, this is very difficult to deal with while it is a dream come true for others. If you are converting a woman in your life, make sure that you are ready and willing to live a female led lifestyle before inviting her into it. If you are looking for a Queen to rule your life, ensure that you have made a firm decision to serve her and you have a strong desire to live this female led lifestyle before building a relationship with a dominant *Love & Obey* woman.

When I made my transition to Queen, my man had to adjust quite a bit to accept my absolute authority over him. He could not question me, criticize me, nor challenge any of my decisions. He simply had to obey me. Whatever I want has to be achieved. Whatever I order has to be obeyed. Whatever I do has to be respected. His life is now totally dedicated to serving me and all of my needs and desires. This lifestyle works for us as a couple. We both have never been happier in our lives.

A Female Led Relationship is part of the incredible and beautiful female authority lifestyle, but be warned you should undoubtedly want it before you read this book. Once you do, you will be well on your way to fully accepting women as your loving authority figures, and you will learn that a man's purpose in life is to submit, love, obey and serve women for the rest of your life, and you will learn that a man's purpose in life is to submit, love, obey and serve women for the rest of your life.

Real Men Worship Women is the title of the book because once you complete reading this, you will learn how to be a gentleman, worship women as your natural superior, and recognize their authority over you. Throughout this book, you will comprehend the importance of the way you address your woman in a female led relationship. In my opinion, there are only three acceptable titles: Mistress, Goddess and Queen.

In my marriage, I allow all three to be used at my man's discretion. This approach is effective and I encourage it for all FLRs. Throughout this book, for simplicity sake, I will refer to the female in a relationship simply as the Queen. I personally like this term the best because of the dictionary definition of the word.

The Dictionary Definition of a Queen.

1: the female ruler of an independent state, especially one who inherits the position by right of birth. 2: a woman eminent in rank, power, or attractions. 3: a goddess or a thing personified as female and having supremacy in a specified realm. 4: the most privileged piece of each color in a set of chessmen having the power to move in any direction.

Relationships are one of the most important and rewarding parts of life, and like anything else worth achieving, it takes effort and work. All relationships require one thing above all else—it must bring happiness to both people involved. The one thing I noticed about successful people was that they worked on every part of their life consistently—physical, financial and relationships. They always had a positive, cheerful attitude about it.

My first book *Love & Obey* surprised me significantly. I was expecting to write a book to discuss my experience with Female Led Relationships. Instead, I unleashed a new movement, one which has grown exponentially. Thousands of couples from around the world are living the *Love & Obey* female led lifestyle and finding great happiness. I had no idea at that time I would be releasing a book at the ultimately changed so many lives.

Women have felt their power growing each year. For many, this "the Future is Female" and "Women Rule" is the new normal. However, in 2017 to 2018, I observed a sharp increase in female empowerment themes in movies, TV, YouTube, governments, corporations and in general households. Everywhere, I had witnessed examples of women taking charge and now it is becoming a worldwide phenomenon in relationships and society. But what I did not realize was the tremendous response from men and how many of them embrace the idea of female superiority and leadership.

The support I received from men speaking about reading *Love & Obey* and practicing it daily, and the hundreds of testimonials I received was overwhelming. Men everywhere told me how they have learned to worship women and how much the book means to them. The excitement toward their partners and enthusiasm for building a female led relationship, in addition to the response and request for a *Love & Obey* guide, book.

Female Led Relationship is the answer to many failing marriages and relationships. Men detailed how *Love & Obey* turned their women around, and made their relationship work or marriage thrive. For many men, the decision to let women lead, love, obey and serve them transformed their relationships from dull to exhilarating and passionate. So, it was only a natural progression for me to write the follow-up book detailing all the rules men should follow to become real gentlemen in a long-lasting Female Led Relationship. Thus, I wrote *Real Men Worship Women, a Gentleman's Guide to Loving Female Authority*.

TABLE OF CONTENTS

The role of obedience in relationships is key to creating a hierarchy of power. Obedience is a form of social influence in which an individual acts in response to a direct order from another individual who is usually an authority figure.

The Love & Obey training system uses audio and/or visual conditioning reinforcers, which a Mistress can deliver quickly and precisely instead of a primary reinforcer, such as a food reward like a cookie.

Why we love our men and need to train them in a loving way. I admire and love men for all their wonderful qualities like loyalty, affection, playfulness, humor, sexuality and zest for life. Nevertheless, men are very different from women.

Remember, that all men are not created equal and some will be decidedly less appealing to women than others. Warning signs and traits that a woman will look out for and how to change them in yourself.

Rewarding your man for good behavior sounds pretty simple—and it is! But to practice the technique effectively, you need to follow some basic guidelines.

Men can be stubborn. Here are some great strategies for teaching a stubborn man. Training a headstrong man can be frustrating. When bad habits refuse to budge, women can wind up feeling frustrated, exhausted and defeated.

The future is female and one day this book will no longer be needed as future generations of women are brought up as the dominant leaders of society and men are taught that their purpose in life is to love, obey and serve women.

CHAPTER 1

> "*I always tell women that there is only one thing they should ever ask from a man. When they ask me what that one thing is, I tell them* OBEDIENCE!"
>
> – Marisa Rudder

Today, women are taking over the world. The signs are everywhere—government, business, society, the media, families and relationships. We all learn our gender roles from social teaching. This includes school, university, the workplace, the media, and from our parents and families. It's learnt from every single interaction we have with the society we live in; from the moment we are born. Since much of society is still largely controlled by men, and influenced by a patriarchal society, a majority of people learn that men should be in control and, despite many social advances, that it is still a woman's place to obey the man and look after the home and children.

This book will teach you why this approach is outdated and does not work in the modern world. A new era of female dominance, occupied by well-educated ambitious women, is the future of the world. We live in a transitional era when women are becoming the dominant force within our society and men are learning to be obedient, happy and submit to female loving authority.

There are many reasons why men and women choose a Female Led Relationship (FLR). In some cases, it's a simple case of an aggressive woman and a passive man, falling into place naturally. In other cases, an alpha man woman recognizing the benefits that my leadership would bring to our relationship and convincing, teaching or reprogramming my man to accept my loving female authority over him and giving him proper direction. These teachings have led me to understand the rules that men must observe to create the best Female Led Relationship.

If men understand these rules early on, then women will experience less stress and anxiety with having to train or reprogram their men on how to behave and serve daily. If men follow the rules then the relationship will be generally positive, rewarding and fulfilling for both genders. When the woman is at peace and more relaxed, she is able to give more love and affection to her man, making him happier than he ever thought possible. Men should love their women as much as themselves. A man who loves his woman loves himself. The need to nourish and cherish ourselves is essential for our well-being and should extend to our relationships.

There are numerous advantages for a relationship where the female is leading the household. This type of relationship ensures that the household benefits from streamlined decision making by the woman. Consensus and acceptance are never good approaches to decision-making as it leads to compromise. Compromise means that neither party is 100 percent happy and any decision is less than optimal. Empowering the wife or girlfriend to make all the decisions brings order, stability and predictability to a relationship. More than anything, it ensures a lack of dispute and argument and this results in a harmonious union.

In addition, men have found that when they assume the role of serving their women, they in fact feel empowered because their women feel much happier and supported for being able to get what they want. The Female Led Relationship is a win-win situation for both. The outcome is less headaches, arguments and disagreements, giving more time to having fun and feeling connected with open communication.

As I've mentioned earlier, I will use the term 'Queen' throughout this book for convenience sake when referring to the woman in the relationship. Men you must submit to your woman as if she was your Queen. From now on, the woman is the head of the husband just like the Queen rules her armies. Your body, and yourself are at her service. Now as armies obey their Queen, a man must obey everything his woman commands.

In the past, the world was run by men but male authoritative relationships are just not as effective. They don't work. The divorce rate is hovering around 50 percent. This is the result of dominant male relationships in the last 50 to 100 years. It is interesting to note that because of the breakdown in the household, with more households run by single moms, the world just evolved to be female led.

Male leadership only leads to conflict, arguments and growing apart. Wars are a male idea. Fighting, in general, is a male idea. Rarely do you see two women getting into a physical altercation. Women in same sex couples are rarely reported for domestic abuse. Why? Because it is part of the male led paradigm. When women feel ignored and pressured by men, they generally start spending more time with friends who allow them to have open communication and feel appreciated.

Many women feel they must suppress a feeling of superiority in fear of upsetting their man's fragile ego. This leads to women feeling underappreciated and stifled. Eventually, a woman who is hiding the need to feel her power becomes depressed, disgruntled and angry.

Men, you don't want to be in a relationship with an angry woman. My simple advice—be obedient to your women, so that even if you have not always obeyed in the past, you must obey her now. Allow yourself to be directed by the commands of your women. When a woman sees you respect her for good choices and intelligent decisions, she will change her conduct and be pleased by your behavior. Then, you will be rewarded. When you reward a woman like a Queen, she will rise to embody a Queen, which means more happiness as you will be proud to be at her side, serving her.

When women are treated like Queens, they will take on the role in their appearance, behavior and outlook, and this will inspire you to be more of a gentleman. You will worship your woman's intelligence, heart and beauty. Your woman will take command of your heart as you submit to her, and she will guide you wisely by the imperishable beauty of her gentle and loving authority over you, which is very precious. For this is how a Gentleman sees his woman, beautifully adorn, inside and out, so it will be easy for him to submit to her. A man must obey his woman in his speech, calling her Goddess, Queen or Mistress.

"Yes, Queen, of course, my Goddess."

"As you command, my Queen."

Just as you address your female leader with a special name, a special name is also given to the male in the relationship. Some common names are slave, pet and baby. I know "slave" is a word that can have negative or derogatory connotations; however, in Love & Obey FLR, it is really complimentary. The reason is that the Love & Obey man is a "Slave to Love" and love is the ultimate and the highest goal to which man can aspire. The salvation of man is through love. I realize that even a man who has nothing left in this world may know bliss, simply in his worship of his loving female authority. So, when your Queen calls you her slave, be honored; her pet, be proud, and her baby, rejoice that you have a Queen who wants you to Love, Obey and Serve her.

And you are to behave appropriately. If you are disobedient, you may be punished as she sees fit. Whatever she says, goes. That's the power of a Female Led Relationship.

I discovered that couples who are in a Female Led Relationship experience more harmony because each person instinctively knows their roles. Your Queen will make sure that what needs to be done in your home is done at the right time, completed in the right order, and is performed well. In any wife-led marriage, she decides what is important for her man to do at any given time. If the man is in agreement, then the relationship is smooth.

However, the challenge occurs when women and men are unsure of their roles and this struggle exists when couples want "equality" in a relationship. I often have this conversation with my friends who are leaders and professionals in their careers. How often does anything get accomplished if everyone in the firm is equal and there is no leader? They usually never agree. It's the same with relationships. Women have been led to believe that the best we can hope for is equality, but equality leads to disagreement.

At some point, someone needs to take leadership in making the decisions and managing the day-to-day activities in the relationship. There can be understandings and "suggestions" by both partners but, in general, leadership is necessary in work at home. The woman must have the final say. Men, submit to their women, as a knight would to his Queen.

Generally, women are more adept leading at home and they make most of the decisions even in traditional marriages, so for men, this is often easily accepted as the way it should be. In FLR, it is enhanced because the woman knows they have a supportive, obedient partner. This obedience only makes the woman happier and more loving to her man.

Have you ever seen the look on your woman's face when you listen to her intently and you participate and encourage her ideas? Women become dynamos when a man supports them. It leads me to think about the idiom "Behind every great woman is a great man." So, obedience to a woman should never be seen as weakness. Strong men know the gift of supporting a strong woman.

This book is going to give you the tools to be able to create that perfect relationship. You're going to enjoy waking up every day, with purpose and direction of knowing that the first thing you must do is to serve your woman as a Queen and reward her as one. Listen obediently to your wife's words. Have nothing to do with any patriarchal or misogynist men, for women have suffered too much already because of them. Women are intelligent, discerning and beautiful, but patriarchal men are often harsh and badly behaved. Your Queen will know what is good for you. She will be wise and she will desire only good things for both of you. You will love and obey her.

There are those who will try to dissuade you, telling you a Female Led Relationship is nonsense results in women rewarding men as slaves. As a matter of fact, the greatest thing a man could do is love and serve a great woman. Referring back to cave men and prehistoric times—it was the man's duty to go out and hunt. Not because the woman was the weaker sex but it was the man's obligation to forage for food and provisions to provide and support the woman and his family.

Today, more and more, men are happy to stay at home and take care of the kids while their wives work. A supportive man makes life easier for a woman who is spending her days at work then coming home to run the household. Think about how much happier she would be when she feels love, respect and admiration from her partner. Happier women are more likely to want to reward you with great sex and you're more likely to get everything you want if your woman is satisfied every single day.

A female led marriage helps you to get past society's unfair demands and expectations of men to always be the leader, the decision maker and the problem solver. But if you are not suited to leadership and you would rather hand over the reins to your Queen, would that not be simpler? Today, men should never be burdened to do things they are not suited for since women in 2020 can do anything a man can do and usually better. Couples have the freedom to choose how to run their own relationships, and more are choosing to be in a Female Led Relationship.

Empowering a woman to lead should not be viewed as negative as it helps to build a stronger, fulfilling relationship. Women are enjoying and welcoming the new role to teach men how to become loving and obedient. I believe that this is the best lifestyle for a truly smooth and happy relationship. Women can teach you more about yourself than you have ever realized or even imagined. She will also share what she needs to be fully stimulated, which means you will please her more. You must understand how to serve her correctly to build intimacy and learn conflict resolution through obedience, as these are all important parts of a relationship that should be addressed daily.

Since the Queen is in charge of the rules of the female led relationship, many sections of this book will need to be read by both of you. Especially if she is a "Queen-in-training" or new to the female led lifestyle. I will make a reference at the beginning of chapters that you both should read to make it easy to share the proper information. Not only should you both read chapters of this book together, you must each show commitment to your roles. Only when both people are truly committed can there be a successful Female Led Relationship.

I encourage you to read this book daily if necessary because it will be a great reminder as to what you need to do every day to serve your Queen. Don't worry, by adhering to the rules, you will have the most interesting, passionate and exciting relationship that you have ever experienced.

CHAPTER 2

> "If a man loves a woman, he will obey her, show
> her love, walk obediently as she commands
> because she only commands him to walk in love!"
>
> – Marisa Rudder

A Fast Start Look at Female Led Relationship Rules.

Relationships are personal, so exactly how you create and live your Female Led Relationship will depend on each couple's personal preferences. However, as a reminder this is truly the kind of relationship you wish for. You must make a commitment to follow and honor the rules to create a successful Female Led Relationship.

Going forward, you don't live for your desires, you live for your Queen's service. In a Female Led Relationship, you will live to love, obey and serve a woman. Your purpose in life will be to make her happy and your happiness will come from how happy you make your woman.

Here is a quick summary of the rules you will follow:

1. Your Queen will give you a list of rules and regulations for you to follow. She will normally write and post this list in the house where you can see and be reminded of them. These set the guidelines for your behavior and they can be general or very detailed. You will be referring to this list on a daily basis for any guidance you may need to determine your behavior.

2. Your Queen is now your sole authority figure. You will show your devotion to her command in many ways. She may choose to refer to you via names such as "slave," "my pet," "my boy" or any other name she wishes to use. She may insist that you bow to her when you first come into her presence. You will also bow when leaving her presence. Many strong women like this and shows her complete attention and devotion. Other gestures such as kissing her hand or her cheek should also be used.

3. You as the man, will no longer refer to your wife or girlfriend with any pet name like "pumpkin," "sugar pie" or "doll face." You will now refer to her as your Queen. Or if you prefer one of these two alternates to Queen; Goddess or Queen. You will also never give another woman attention while in your Queen's presence unless given permission to do so. You will also not speak until your Queen allows you to. Men should be seen and not heard.

4. Personal hygiene is extremely important. Shaving, ensuring your clothes are clean and pressed, doing the laundry, ensuring the bed is made each morning, and maintaining a clean and tidy area at all times. You want to show your Queen you are deserving of her utmost respect. Even small actions like putting the toilet seat down after using it will go a long way to show that you care and are also attentive. Breakfast in bed, running her bath, getting her favorite soap or dessert; you must learn to think ahead and surprise her. You must remove all

misogynistic, patriarchal or machismo thoughts or language from your speech. You must be submissive and polite to all women and this will be required at all times.

5. The domestic chores will now become your duties, unless your Queen enjoys the task, like cooking. You will be required to do all the house cleaning and chores, including washing and ironing the clothes, cooking, washing the dishes, cleaning the toilet and bath, and all other domestic work in the house. The woman may set out a roster of weekly chores for the man to do each week. Sometimes a Queen likes to cook or even do some housework but that would be her choice and is totally at her discretion. You are her servant now.

6. Your Queen will control your clothing. I believe this to be an important area to address in a *Love & Obey* FLR. There are three reasons. First, it enforces your Queen's authority over you and ensures you wear clothing she will enjoy seeing you in. Regarding status, people react to clothing as symbols of position and power or of lowly status. Different women employ different techniques here but the key is demonstration of the status differential. The woman is the General, the Boss and the Queen. The man is the private, the admin assistant and the knight. We therefore need to dress men according to what we as Queens desire. I even like to keep my man naked at home. I like this approach and adopt it—or variations of it—many times because my husband works out and takes care of his body so he is sexy to me. When we go out, I prefer him to dress in a sophisticated, hip and stylish manner. For me being naked and me choosing his wardrobe helps to strip away any nasty macho traits of independence. I deal with this issue with clothing and in every phase of the relationship to create my female led reality. Finally, it's just very pleasant to see a stylishly dressed man or a naked man if he has a good physique.

7. My first rule is that sex is now for your woman's pleasure and your focus should be 100 percent on satisfying and pleasuring your Queen. Your pleasure must strictly come from the amount of arousal you give your woman. The Queen absolutely controls all sexual activity. Within the relationship, I go for "orgasm denial" as a powerful form of chastity. Control of his orgasms and ejaculations is a power control mechanism. In my case, I allow his sexual release once or twice a month. I know this is very liberal for many women in the female led lifestyle, but I am good-hearted.

   My man also knows that he is DEFINITELY not allowed to experience orgasm without my permission. As a rule, I am the one who decides where, when and what kind of sex we are having. The Queen will also decide about threesomes, cuckolding and group sex, and whether she desires it or not. You now must obey her desires. I can tell you that I am a big fan of oral sex and I have it performed on me daily. I rarely if ever, give my man a blow job. I don't enjoy it and I don't have to reciprocate, but he is enthusiastic to perform oral sex on me and he does it on my command.

8. In many Female Led Relationships today, the man is a stay-at-home dad and the woman has a successful career as a doctor, lawyer or corporate executive. If the woman is the money earner and/or better at managing money, then she should take control over the finances. If the man also works but earns less, the man should turn his earnings over to his Queen to manage. This doesn't mean keeping him broke or denying him his little treats, it just means the Queen is in control. For example, I buy my husband special "rewards" like tickets for live sporting events that I sometimes attend. I then give him an allowance so he can buy coffee, a drink or sandwich.

I think a limited petty cash allowance is a good idea for men. It keeps them coming back and asking for more money from his Queen. If the man is wealthy or earns most of the money and is better at managing money, then he should handle managing money; however, the Queen should have access to all accounts. The Queen should also be in charge of major purchases and overall spending of the money.

9. the outings will entail. For example, if you are going out to eat and to watch a movie, the Queen will decide which restaurant to eat at and which movie you will watch. She will decide all other social activities as well and you will cheerfully join her.

10. Obedience to your Queen is the foundation of any Female Led Relationship. Strict female discipline is therefore an important element of the relationship to ensure that you always obey your Queen's commands. Verbal discipline and the removal of rights is the way I prefer to control my man; however, some physical discipline can be beneficial such as spanking or slapping. More discipline is required during your initial male training and after you are well behaved, some occasional reinforcement discipline will be needed from time to time. Breaches of obedience should always be met with very strict discipline to send a clear message that your Queen is the boss and you serve her.

11. Language is an important aspect to changing behavior. The proper words must be used when addressing your Queen. Males should use appropriate titles such as Queen, Goddess, or my Queen. My husband addresses me as Queen and Goddess. I like having my husband bow his head when he first sees me and when he leaves my presence. It is also important to thank your Queen when she gives you a command or she allows you to sexually please her. Respectful language is a constant

reminder of the status difference between you and your woman in the relationship and ensures your constant obedience.

CHAPTER 3

> "A man must obey his Queen in everything she commands. A man must try to please her all the time, not just when she is watching him. A man must serve her sincerely because of his love and respect for her."
>
> – Marisa Rudder

An excellent woman who believes in loving female authority over men is hard to find. She is far more precious than diamonds and gold. A man must trust in her and he will have a happy and fulfilling life. Love and obey her and she will give you love all the days of your life. When you put your woman on a pedestal, she will rise to embody that role. *Love & Obey* women feel respected and desired every day, so they work on maintaining an image to inspire you and everyone she meets. She will generally use her charm and confidence to demand respect. A *Love & Obey* woman is wise when she speaks and she leads with kindness and loving female authority will be on her tongue.

For you, this means you will receive a lot of her attention and wisdom. You will learn how to respect and treat all women. In my first book, I laid out the basics of a Female Led Relationship and how to create one. Now, I will dive into what the rules are for men to follow. There are a number of steps you will need to take to develop a successful Female Led Relationship or FLR. Although each woman will have her own unique touches to add, the fundamentals will remain the same. The rules will be divided between everything you should do at home, out in public, on special occasions and in any conflict resolution.

These rules need to be adhered to succeed in your Female Led Relationship. In the beginning there will be conflict as you will be challenged every day to set aside your own wishes and typical male programmed behavior and approaches to doing things. Now you will be following your Queen's rules and decisions. You should give yourself time to learn the rules and follow them daily. Practice makes perfect. The more you follow the rules, the more obedient and submissive to your woman you will become. It will soon become natural and you will gain much more enjoyment for your relationship.

Repetition is a key to learning so here are more on the rules for you to follow at home:

1. Your Queen makes the rules and you must obey them always. No exceptions.

2. Your Queen creates a list of rules, chores and regulations for you to follow. They should be reviewed regularly together. This helps to set the expectations and parameters of the relationship.

3. Establish yourself as a masculine "Knight" figure. She will be your Queen and you are her Knight, which means your purpose in life is to support her and be at her side. You should address her as "Queen" and "Goddess" as much as possible.

4. Be respectful of her wishes and desires at all times, even when you disagree. Allow her to express her views and

listen intently. This is not always easy for men since most will want to go into a defensive, guarded and silent position when confronted. Generally, women just want to be heard and they often need a good listener. So, be a confidant for her who she can discuss any issues with openly.

5. Keep up with your chores without the need for constant reminders. If she decides that your duties are taking out the garbage and doing the dishes, do them each day without having to be reminded. Your goal is to reduce her responsibility with the domestic chores. For some women, the household chores will be divided between both of you. But for others, they may decide that you do all household chores. You should establish this right from the start. In my case, I enjoy cooking and doing the dishes, so my man must get used to doing all the other chores in the house. It is also important for you to try to anticipate what your Queen may want.

6. Be attractive to your woman as much as possible. I believe this to be one of the most important areas to address in any FLR. Present yourself the way she wants to see you. If she likes a beard, grow one. If she enjoys seeing you clean-shaven and in good shape, then do what you can to keep her attraction toward you as much as possible. Staying attractive and practicing good hygiene are key. Women don't always say it, but bad breath, farting and bad smells can turn them off. They may not criticize you out of love, but it tends to be an issue.

Analyze your presentation skills. You never see a knight or head of an army show himself in front of the Queen looking like the court jester or the gardener. So, take your cues from your Queen and present yourself in a way that is attractive to her. Women respond to their men putting some interest in their appearance. They love a visually appealing man on their arm. You're now her arm candy.

7. Your Queen will have complete control of sex, and all focus on pleasure is for the Queen. Men must learn that sex is for the Queen' pleasure. You will need to learn to serve her needs. If you don't know how to perform everything your Queen wants, then you must learn. Read books, watch videos on YouTube—whatever you need to do to master how to pleasure her until she is satisfied. You will not have sexual pleasure without your woman's permission. You will only be allowed to orgasm with her permission. And unless she wants you to serve another person, you will only serve her. You will listen to your woman and you will obey her voice.

8. Engage in discussions about what ultimately turns her on. When I was younger, I felt so unsatisfied that my mind often began to wander as I just tried to get through bad sex. This was destructive in many ways because it was not fair to my partner as he had no idea I was not pleased, and I never encouraged open communication about what I needed. In a selfish way, I just expected men to know.

    Now, older, I realize this is key. Open communication about how to pleasure her is extremely important and it can make or break a relationship. Most men don't realize it but the tongue is mightier than the penis. I believe that when a man regularly performs oral sex on a female, it increases her pleasure. It also increases his desire and need to be obedient and submissive to his *Love & Obey* Queen. You will need to be an expert at performing oral sex on your Queen. You will also have to be trained to control your orgasms until you are allowed to ejaculate. You must learn to perform for your Queen until she is totally satisfied and tells you to stop.

9. Your Queen must be the one who decides when, where and how you have sex. She may decide to put you in chastity, or demand that you come ONLY when she commands. These are things you will need to discuss with her in an open conversation. If she forbids you from masturbating, you must stop. This is the difference with a Female Led Relationship; you must take your orders from your Queen. Any argument and objections means you are not really practicing FLR. Orgasm denial for men seems scary at first but you will learn to appreciate it, and holding on to your sexual energy will make you a better, disciplined man.

10. You must orally pleasure your Queen first during sex if this is what she desires, and you will learn to be good at it. Women generally need a lot of foreplay and arousal before they can fully enjoy sex. Too many men rush this process and women are left counting the minutes and waiting for it to be over. This cannot happen in a Female Led Relationship. You must learn what your Queen desires and do it every time. The key is to ask questions and listen intently.

11. Flattery will get you everywhere. Compliment your Queen whenever you can. I was always amazed at how many strong women never received compliments from their men and craved the attention. People just assumed they were super women and didn't require any bolstering. However, like all human beings, they wished for someone to notice their efforts and this usually fell on the shoulders of their partners. So, as the person who is most likely to support your Queen, part of your daily task will be to compliment and keep her in a good mood.

12. Most men assume women don't want sex as much as a man does until they meet one who does. Your biggest problem will come from keeping up with her unleashed desires. The truth is that many women don't want sex

often because they are usually being used, and are not being satisfied by selfish, untrained men. So, even if you don't think this sounds fair now, the good news is that when you start focusing 100 percent on her pleasure during sex, and she knows that sex is for her pleasure, she will want it much more often. Typically, within six months the woman will want intercourse daily. You will be having a lot of sex, and you will often enjoy yourself. Most women will see to that one way or another.

13. Make sure your Queen is having real orgasms. It is no secret that many women fake it. Pretending is not something they enjoy doing. As part of the patriarchal society, women always felt that it was a blow to a man's ego if they did not have an orgasm. But, in a Female Led Relationship, I consider this to be a failure. You cannot fake serve a Queen. Either you serve her or do not. Part of a Female Led Relationship is understanding what will incite an orgasm by paying attention to everything she instructs. Read books, get toys, costumes, candles, bubble bath—whatever you can to put her in the mood and ensure she is pleasured. This is a win-win situation for both of you.

14. Allow your Queen to control the finances if she desires so. Many strong women have managed many aspects of their lives and they are much better at controlling spending and savings. If the Queen delegates the finances because you are a pro, then that would be the only time it is permissible. The Queen will normally request to make the major purchases for the household and avoid giving the man money, which can make him feel empowered and independent. This doesn't mean keeping a man in poverty or denying him any rewards, it just means overall control. When the woman controls the finances, she has more authority and power; thus, the man naturally becomes

more submissive and obedient, and is able to get his allowance.

15. Your Queen controls social activities. There is no more going out with the boys four nights a week your Queen will decide on a schedule of what is appropriate. This includes what times you both will be home, and when dinner will be ready, etc.

   Social activities will be decided by the Queen. It does not mean you cannot ask permission to go out with your friends, but you cannot assume this is ok. The point of a Female Led Relationship is to relate. You must spend time together. Too many couples are just existing and shacking up for the sake of convenience. In a Female Led Relationship, this can't happen because for you to give control of your life over to your woman, you better truly love, respect and enjoy spending time with her.

   Merely shacking up, going to work, and avoiding spending quality time together is the beginning of the death of a relationship. This was in my experience and what I witnessed with thousands of couples. Sometimes I could predict the break up years before. At times I observe a couple's behavior together at a party and I could predict the state of their relationship. I was rarely wrong.

16. At home, your Queen decides what shows to watch and you give her the remote. If she wants to allow you to watch football or any show you would like, you will need to ask her permission. You must never keep the remote for yourself, and prevent her from watching what she wants. In addition, you will get the snacks for TV watching. No longer is the Queen slaving to bring food to you. If this is something she enjoys, only then is it permitted. When the Queen is relaxing as she watches TV, you will ask if she needs anything, and get it immediately, even if it means going out to the store.

Real Men Worship Women

17. During potential arguments at home, you will always be respectful and calmly talk it out. You will allow the Queen to have her say first, then you can explain your side. You will never interrupt the Queen while she is speaking to you. With that said, all conflicts must be approached with open communication. If you offend the Queen, then you need to apologize.

I usually decide little fun ways for my man to apologize. I might make him crawl on the floor, kiss my feet, and then "hee-haw" like a jackass until he apologizes. I find those very amusing punishments and it gets the point across to him in a harmless and painless way that he was acting like an ass. The point is that you must be respectful to the Queen at all times.

18. Every time you enter the room and your Queen is present, you will address her. At no time should you come home or wake up in the morning and fail to say hello. I noticed a very rude practice in which many couples fail to even address their partner in the morning or when returning home, either because they are tired or do not feel that these little niceties are necessary. In a Female Led Relationship, it is considered rude and unacceptable if you fail to say "hello," "good morning" or "good evening" to the Queen. The same goes for her; she must always address you as well. Couples ignoring each other is paving the way for disaster in the relationship. Big problems always start with small issues, which are often overlooked.

21

CHAPTER 4

Men need to be taught correct behavior by women. So, both you and your Queen need to keep open communication. She must review the rules with you on a regular basis and you must adhere. FLR relationships may seem normal to an outsider—just a dominant woman leading her man and the household. However, what you are doing privately is creating a relationship hierarchy, setting up a structure, and establishing a successful Female Led Relationship.

The following are some additional steps I found to be helpful during the training period. You and your Queen should review these:

1. **Positive learning with rewards**. Positive learning with rewards comes straight out of operant conditioning which is a method which rewards good behavior. The difference between loving FLR and dominatrix is that behavior is rewarded not punished as much. I found that providing mini rewards for a man who goes out of his way

to please me is one of the best ways to keep both people happy. Affection, praise, compliments little gifts and of course sexual rewards all can be used as positive reinforcement of good behavior. In normal relationships this is not emphasized and both people feel ignored. The number of times, I tried to cook a great meal for my previous partners, do chores or dress up for seduction only to be ignored and met with a lukewarm reaction which was extremely disappointing. In some relationships, I found it more interesting to hang out with friends than to be with my partner because I never received compliments, praise or positive remarks. So, I know what it's like for men now, in a Female Led Relationship and how important mini rewards are.

2. **Coaching in the bedroom.** It is extremely important in a FLR that your Queen tell you and openly communicate what she likes and dislikes in the bedroom and coaches you on how to please her. This is mandatory, not only to ensure there is open communication but for both of you to feel attention. There is nothing worse than waking up one day for your partner to say, you never satisfied her. But also, that she never provided guidance. A relationship is a two-way street and requires communication and action on both sides. Your Queen must be authoritative and firm but still kind. I usually demonstrate what I need and then and guide my partner, providing instructions where necessary. A *Love and Obey* woman how to take charge of a relationship and provide you with the necessary guidance. You must be open to all of her suggestions and try to deliver the best you can. "Happy Wife Happy Life" there is truth in this saying for a reason. You want to ensure that your Queen is happy and you should be communicating openly so that you know if things are off track.

3. Mutual awareness of lifestyle. For a Queen who is new to this lifestyle, it will be important for you to have her read my first book *Love & Obey* so she becomes familiar with the lifestyle. There is nothing worse than a man who gets excited to get into this lifestyle but your Queen has no idea. You don't want to throw it at her. Rather, slowly get her to be excited by the concept, and understanding the lifestyle and what the expectations are for the both of you. Reviewing the rules in both books together helps to ensure you are both on the same page.

4. Some couples like the idea of mini punishments for bad behavior. Where loving FLR involves positive reinforcement for good behavior, non-physical punishment can also be used. For me, punishment is the withdrawal of privileges or verbal discipline. BDSM/FEMDOM or extremely cruel behavior of any kind toward men is not permitted in loving female led relationships. Think of how you would reward a beloved pet, like a dog. You would train your pet and discipline your pet when behaving badly but you will also spoil and shower your pet with a lot of love and affection when he is good. To mistreat a pet is to create a monster in the future. Many dog owners especially learn this. Training a man in an FLR is very similar.

Those parts of BDSM and extreme domination where the goal is to savagely beat men, lock them in dog cages, or worst, is not acceptable. They may be part of fetishes, but for building a long-term successful relationship, I feel they are destructive. You don't get close to a man who you need to paddle, beat and cage daily. A Female Led Relationship is about building a loving relationship like all others, to last and be a great experience for both people. Light non-physical punishment is acceptable because some couples enjoy this idea of the Queen taking away a reward as a mini punishment to coerce good behavior. Some examples I have used are TV privileges revoked, watching sports are banned, as well as doing extra chores. It ends up being fun for both the Queen and her man, but it should be used lightly.

5. There are many ways that an FLR might work for you, and it depends on what your Queen wants. However, whatever the level of *Love & Obey* Queenship in a relationship, teaching and re-teaching of your man is necessary because of the way we are brought up in a man-dominated social environment. We need to retrain and put *Love & Obey* Queenship in the forefront, one relationship at a time, one family, one city. Although we can see this changing, it's far too slow and so we need to think of women, such as me, as global change-makers in the vanguard of change. A large amount of teaching and ongoing reinforcement is necessary to achieve a successful and fully functioning FLR, even in situations where the man is accepting and desirous of Queenship.

In my own relationship, my man is a confident and assertive person when dealing with the outside world and other men, but totally submissive to me, and this is surprisingly common in FLRs. However, whether you are a man with an assertive or a submissive personality or, as is more likely, somewhere in between, the objective is the same. A Female Led Relationship will bring happiness and more love into your life.

Here are some simple rules of the *Love & Obey* Female Led Relationship that I use in my own household:

1. I make most of the decisions for both of us, and delegate some decision-making when I know that my man has more expertise in a particular area.

2. I am always rewarded like a Queen all day, every day—in bed and out of it. I am usually referred to as "Queen or Goddess" when my man addresses me. He typically

introduces me in public and says, "This is my Goddess, Marisa."

3. Our sex life has improved enormously, and all sex, as I mentioned before, is for my pleasure. My man performs oral sex on me virtually every day and I completely control when he is allowed to orgasm.

4. I do the cooking because I like being in control of the kitchen and some of the housework, or I have our housekeeper do it under my direction. My man does any chores that I command him to do.

5. All of our money is mine and under my control. He knows that he works for me and I am the CEO of our life. We only spend on what I approve of.

6. Our relationship runs smoothly and we rarely argue, and arguments that do occur are quickly resolved in my favor. I make him crawl to my feet and apologize, or even "hee-haw" like a donkey after an argument to show him that he has acted like a jackass by defying my loving authority.

7. My man and I train in the gym four to five times a week and we eat a very healthy diet. I tell him which body parts to focus on working out and how much he can eat. He is thinner and more in shape than when we met and has never looked better. We are a fit couple who focus on sexual pleasure rather than gluttony with food as a form of pleasure.

8. Our relationship is how I want it to be. We are a strong couple, and he is more affectionate and loving, and we are both healthier and happier than ever before.

9. My man and I have enjoyed an FLR relationship for more than five years now and we are more in love than when we met.

10. My own relationship with my man works very well, and all the successful relationships I have witnessed in my family and in life, in general, have been female led. So, the advice that I give is meant to help you achieve a similar successful Female Led Relationship.

CHAPTER 5

"A Man must love his woman and always obey her
requirements, rules, regulations and commands."

– Marisa Rudder

There is importance of understanding the difference between being a Queen in an FLR and being a dominatrix in the BDSM/FEMDOM lifestyle. Let's start with the biggest misconception of a female led relationship. People assume you are becoming a dominatrix and your man is a submissive slave, but that is not the case. Yes, your woman may punish you (as men have punished women in the past) if you do not obey her commands, and if you do not make her life more the life she desires with each passing day. Remember, in an FLR, a man must look beyond his own interests and succumb to his Queen's instead since her needs and desires are now his number one priority in life.

Let's start from the beginning. What is a dominatrix? She is a woman who takes the dominant role in BDSM/FEMDOM activities, and not involved in a loving Female Led Relationship. This book is for men and women who want to lead but do not want to be a dominatrix/submissive and practice BDSM/FEMDOM. A dominatrix is typically a paid professional and this term is used primarily within the BDSM/FEMDOM scene. So, be clear to yourself and your friends. You are not a dominatrix and your husband is not a submissive worm; you are a loving female authority and he is your obedient gentleman. Now, that is not to say that you can't have a little "BDSM/FEMDOM fantasy play time," of course you can, but it should be all in good fun and nobody gets hurt.

In the world of a loving FLR, the female is simply the leader. Think of it this way, in the military, there is a general and then there are the soldiers. Your Queen is the female general and you are the soldier. You can be yourself, or you can even be macho, but you are always her soldier and she is always your general. Your Queen is in charge; think of a Queen and her three musketeers. They are brave, tough and strong but they love, obey and serve their Queen. She simply becomes the *Love & Obey* Queen in your relationship, the general, and you have chosen to be her mate, her soldier.

Your Queen leads you as a man and you obey like a good soldier should. One side-note, a female led relationship can be used for people of any sexual orientation. A leadership role as General is not limited by your sexual orientation and does not necessarily limit the genders of your partner/soldiers. However, *Love & Obey* is generally geared toward heterosexual relationships.

In the *Love & Obey* world, the role of a Queen does not involve physical pain toward the man. Instead, a *Love & Obey* Queen's domination is typically verbal; your Queen gives the commands (she is the Boss or the General) and demands your obedience to her orders and your good behavior. Like a good soldier, you must obey and serve her commands. You must strive to "complete the mission" and fulfill the wishes of your female general.

The confusion in the world of a Female Led Relationship and BDSM/FEMDOM comes from the fact that the woman is now in a dominant role and honestly does tend to become a much more sexualized woman. More so than a woman with a traditional man or jointly led relationship, but the similarity between the two lifestyles ends at that point. The loving FLR in this book is chosen by the woman and the man because of their personal preference for the female to take charge and lead in a loving way that benefits both partners and maintains both their dignity and self-respect.

The concept is the opposite of many of the dark conventions of the BDSM/FEMDOM scene. I use the term "Queen" because Queen is a salutation of respect, such as "May I introduce to you, Queen Marisa." Although the female has dominance in a loving female led relationship, she is not cruel and mean. FemDom refers to BDSM/FEMDOM activities in which the dominant partner may be female but she is not loving, compassionate nor respectful of the man's dignity. This fetish culture is becoming more prevalent in Western media, as depicted in TV and film and many men desire this sexual fantasy, but it is not a part of the loving Female Led Relationship lifestyle that I teach.

Let's look back in history; dominatrix is the feminine form of the Latin word dominator, a ruler or lord, and was originally used in a non-sexual sense. The use of the word in English dates back to at least 1561. Its earliest recorded use in today's common and modern sense, as a female dominant in BDSM/FEMDOM, dates back only to the 1960's. It was initially coined to describe a woman who provides punishment-for-pay. When Bruce Roger's paperback *The Bizarre Love Makers* entered more popular mainstream knowledge following the 1976 film *Dominatrix Without Mercy*. Some aspects of the dominatrix may overlap with the *Love & Obey* Queen and increase confusion. For example, the body language of the dominatrix and the *Love & Obey* Queen is frequently represented by the use of strong, dominant body-language, but for me, both evolved from the dominant posturing in the animal world and it is perfectly natural.

Although the term "dominatrix" was not used, the classic example in literature of the female dominant-man submissive relationship is portrayed in the 1870 novella *Venus in Furs* by Austrian writer Leopold von Sacher-Masoch. The term masochism was later derived from the author's name.

The practices of the modern-day, professional dominatrix in real-life is considered by many to be a "bizarre lifestyle." Women who engage in female domination typically promote and title themselves under the term "dominatrix." That's why I don't use this term. I prefer Goddess and Queen. In film, the dominatrix is depicted wearing leather (latex and rubber) catsuits. In comic books, such as Catwoman, the catsuit represents the independent woman capable of "kick-ass" moves and antics over men, and the outfit enables complete freedom of movement. It also simultaneously obstructs physical penetration and access by the man, symbolically showing female control over sex. It sends a message of "You can look at me and get excited but you can't touch."

This type of leather, latex or rubber fashion has become increasingly popular in modern society. This fashion is enjoyed by women in female led relationships as well, and is used to send the same message. The woman is in charge and runs the show. Sexual access to women has become a major socio-political issue and has created the #meToo movement. The sexual assaults on prominent celebrities, business leaders and politicians have sent a clear message of a women's control. Women control their bodies, women control sex and if you want it, and you will do what we say. Women are now in charge of heterosexual men because sex is a powerful force of nature and can sway a man's behavior.

I believe wearing a provocative outfit like a latex dress, fishnet stockings, thigh high boots or stiletto heels, and playing a fantasy game with your man is exciting and adds a great deal to a relationship. In human sexuality, it is fantastic to broaden and mutually explore female domination and man submission roles, emotions and activities, and even better once you act them out with a willing partner. It is exhilarating to take a non-traditional or opposing role. For example, in many Female Led Relationships, there is often a sexual switch, and females are often on top during sex, and generally receive much more oral sex than their male partners.

The man usually only receives oral sex as a very special reward for very good behavior and only if the female wants to perform it, while the female may receive oral sex almost daily and on demand. The switch in roles from the man demanding a "blow job" to the woman demanding "pussy licking" is a major power shift that occurs only in a Female Led Relationship. In my experience, when females take control of the sex life, which is essential in a Female Led Relationship, a man is typically trained to perform oral sex on a female on a regular basis and the result is that he learns to enjoy it. The man eventually accepts that sex is for the female's pleasure and that his pleasure is derived from "servicing" his Queen as she desires.

Women in female led also accepts the idea that men are here to service and perform services for them. This is the major gender power shift and man-female role reversal that makes Female Led Relationships so new and exciting. Sexual domination is a good tool that can be used by women to naturally take a more dominant role in the relationship, and make the man more submissive and obedient. For this reason, sexual positions change from the man on top to the female on top during sex, which supports the psychological role that the female is now running the show. In real life, this creates a new power dynamic and makes life fresh, new and exciting when used in love making and the kind of sexual domination that eliminates "bedroom boredom" that occurs in long-term relationships and spices things up tremendously.

This type of sexual role reversal is becoming acceptable in mainstream society. The dominant female character and the submissive-obedient man is the new rising star in popular culture. This is definitely a positive change in behavior of the female led subculture that owes a lot of gratitude to the BDSM/FEMDOM community. The issue with BDSM/FEMDOM for me is the degradation, demeaning, cruel, and abusive behavior that belittles a man and makes him totally worthless. "Sissification" and other forms of man humiliation and abuse are simply taken too far in my opinion in the hard core BDSM/FEMDOM community.

I am simply saying that the *Love & Obey* female led lifestyle does not include emasculating men and taking away their manhood. I am proposing a change in what is considered manly. Men can be modern day gentlemen who worship their women as their superiors. Women are the leaders and men must love and obey them. Men must do as women say, which clearly allows some women to dominate in the classic BDSM/FEMDOM style. I have a great deal of followers in this BDSM/FEMDOM world on my social media, and I am not judging anyone. To each their own, and if you are a consenting adult, I say live and let live. I am merely offering a form of FLR, which can be respectful of the man and rewards him more like a beloved human than an abused man.

The common link between a *Love & Obey* female led relationship and the BDSM/FEMDOM world is that the woman is the boss. The women dominate the relationship and the man obeys. Perhaps one easy way to look at it is "the Wizard of Oz approach" in female led relationships in which there are good witches and bad witches. Each man must choose whether he wants to be ruled by a "good witch" or a "bad witch" and each woman must decide which role she wants to play. Naturally, there are varying degrees to how much or how little punishment, humiliation, sissification and discipline each woman adds to her relationship. Some add a lot of BDSM and some add a little *Love & Obey*. Again, it is up to each consenting adult couple to decide for themselves. As they say, "Whatever floats your boat."

I do enjoy fun and games and "fantasy role play," but I do have some issues with the bad witch BDSM/FEMDOM lifestyle. My issue is with the real destruction of the man psyche in terms of humiliation, corporal abuse and ultimately the de-construction of a man's masculinity. I do not "hate" men. I love and enjoy men and their masculine qualities (not just their penis), but at the same time, I do demand a transformation of the patriarchal or misogynistic man into a gentleman who worships women. I want my man to be all man, worshipping me and behaving in a chivalrous manner that is pleasing to me. I believe in modern day chivalry that requires a man to live in the service of his Queen.

Women should be controlling the relationship and they should be dominant, but in the *Love & Obey* relationship, women are respectful of their man's needs. Most men enjoy this *Love & Obey* exchange of sexual and lifestyle authority to the female. Therefore, I encourage women to lead with responsibility, control and compassion, so they can achieve the ultimate goal of a loving and mutually respectful relationship.

Still, common factors remain between a dominatrix and a *Love & Obey* Queen. Both may come from multiple different backgrounds, but a considerable number of these women are well-educated and smart, with a recent survey in New York revealing that 39 percent had attended graduate school, including prestigious institutions such as Columbia University. Thus, women in Female Led Relationships tend to be well-educated and intelligent, so they are well suited to lead men.

I simply prefer the *Love & Obey* soft approach to a more loving and respectful style of Queenship. I reach out to couples who desire Female Led Relationships and try to share my book *Love & Obey*, simply showing them that they can lead in a loving, compassionate and respectful way. I am hoping to convert as many couples as possible to my philosophy of loving female authority.

However, for many women, their role as a dominatrix is not really about a relationship at all. They are professionals who advertise their services online. Many women actively offer professional domination services. Most of these professionals practice in metropolitan cities like New York, Los Angeles, and London—with as many as 200 women working as dominatrices in Los Angeles alone. They argue that they are fulfilling a need for men who have fetishes, and take pride in their technical ability to perform complex BDSM practices, such as bondage, suspension, torture roleplay, and corporal punishment, which require a high degree of knowledge and competency to safely supervise.

For example, the use of a "safeword" is usually given to the male partner to prevent the dominant from overstepping physical and emotional boundaries. The "safeword" is especially important because the dominant may not be aware of a boundary until it is crossed.

Many of these dominatrix women are really all about financial domination, or findom, a fetish in which a submissive is aroused by sending money or gifts to a dominatrix at her instruction. In some cases, these interactions are only performed using the Internet, and the dominatrix and the submissive never meet. So, it's really just about the money, and has nothing to do with a real-life relationship. To differentiate, what I am teaching is a real "lifestyle," a real, loving relationship, typically between a man and a woman. The professional dominatrix really is not involved in my world of building happy female led couples.

This book is not about the "professional BDSM business and FemDom money making world" of the dominatrix. I am trying to teach women how to use *Love & Obey* Queenship and behavioral training techniques within their own private lives and relationships, to improve the world. I believe women are superior to men and that men are better off in an obedient role that gives their life purpose by serving women. In my experience, women are much better at running relationships than men, and

I want both to experience the real joy and happiness in their private relationships that comes from a real FLR. Men can be "gentle", obedient and submissive to women. They can also still be manly and play sports, hunt, fish, ride motorcycles, drive pickup trucks, shoot guns and do all sorts of masculine activities, but when it comes to their relationship, they submit to their women and are always obedient.

CHAPTER 6

> "A man must obey his woman and live by her rules, then he will become her special treasure from among all the other men on earth; for a man should belong to his woman."
>
> – Marisa Rudder

Living in a real-life, real-world FLR, I see how men thrive in female led relationships because even the most alpha 6'4 athletic man is more comfortable worshiping the woman he loves than being in charge. It may not seem like it, but the truth is, dating and marriage are based on the man being accommodating to the female's desires and fulfilling them. Dating is all about bringing pleasure and excitement to a woman to win her over, so she will allow you to have sex with her. Whether this attentiveness is outwardly expressed is up to the woman who naturally is in charge since she is the object of the man's yearning.

Everyone wants to be loved and men want to be loved just as much as women. Men also want to have sex, and when the woman controls the sex, she commands the man's wish to have her feminine delights. He will do what needs to be done to win her affection, so he can be intimate with her, and perhaps on a higher level that sex can blossom into love. Females lead most relationships simply because we are "love" for men. We set the expectations and the rules that the man must follow to successfully gain the female's affection, love and become his sex partner, life partner or wife.

Remember the underlying fever and desire of the first few weeks of dating? We know the man wants to have sex with us, and we must decide when we will allow it. Some women even have rules about when they will have sex with a man, in an effort to send the right signals. "I enjoy sex but I don't want you to think I give it too easily." Few relationships are officially recognized as "female led" but make no mistake about it, as long as women have what the man wants, women are in control. The female is in control of the sex life because a man must always have the woman's consent for sex. Otherwise, it's called sexual abuse or worse yet, felony rape!

For most women, controlling the sexual activity in a marriage is natural and done in a conscious manner and most women limit their husband's sexual access after the dating stage until "death do us part." He may want sex three times every day but very few women are willing to agree to accommodate this sort of male sexual desire.

Even young females shape their man's sexual boldness. Most female's like to make sex "a special event" and not an everyday chore. Using sex as a reward—the blow job after receiving a beautiful gift, or after the man performs a loving action—is common for women. In addition, limiting penetration to a certain amount of times each month gradually transfers sexual control to the wife. Women know, a horny man is an attentive man. Keeping a man horny is a very good place to keep a relationship. Most women try to always keep men aroused. It is also a very good power to use when teaching your man self-control. The truth is men think "they are all that" in bed and that they want sex all the time, but if they are allowed to have intercourse all the time. they would quickly cross a threshold and lose interest. When men satisfy a female's desire and focus all sexual gratification on her in a Female Led Relationship, men quickly realize women want it more than men. Typically, females even those who do not think of themselves as dominant Queens usually take charge in the bedroom. Controlling what he wants—access to pussy and denying male orgasm is a key way to maintain rein over the man. Women are natural leaders because "She controls the pussy, so she controls the man!"

In the past, and still in some backward thinking patriarchal countries, women are forced by cultural norms to have sex whenever the man desires it. This takes away female power and makes women adopt a mental attitude of only performing out of a sense of duty. A man's unchecked sexual demands are a recipe for disaster. Most women become frigid, suffer from anorgasmia or become uninterested in sex only when their own sexual needs are suppressed and not addressed by the man. The end result of a man who does not pleasure his female is that she shuts down sexually. This happens even in Western Society, and that's why men think they have stronger sexual desires than women. This is simply not true. Women have higher sex drives then men— WHEN THEIR PLEASURE COMES FIRST.

Unfortunately, in the past and still in some archaic- thinking countries, women remain sexually compliant and give their husbands what they want out of obligation and fear of punishment. Female Led Relationships end this situation for women, and can actually make life easier on their men. Men get more sex in a Female Led Relationship because the female wants it more, and because it becomes an enjoyable source of pleasure for her. However, *Love & Obey* women know that male orgasm denial is key.

The man cannot be allowed to orgasm every time you have sex, or even regularly. He must be trained to control himself and focus on stimulating the female until she climaxes. This orgasm denial is one reason that performing oral sex exclusively on women, several days a week, is quite common in a Female Led Relationship. It keeps the man "horny" and conscientious, while the women increase her pleasure and relaxation.

The reality is that if a woman is properly pleasured by an attentive and somewhat skilled lover, she will develop a strong, pleasurable bond with the man and would crave lovemaking regularly. Couples also realize the passion and sexual experience will be far greater for both partners when the women's pleasure is put in the forefront and remains the central focus of attention.

Believe it or not, it is stressful for a man to constantly feel pressured to be erect and it becomes tougher as they age. Although teenage men with raging hormones may be able to get erections and ejaculate over and over in a single day, men, even in their thirties, cannot perform at this level. Most men will deny this because of their huge egos and false belief in their amazing sexual prowess. Witness a man who cannot "get it up" and they become completely humiliated and ashamed, no matter how much we tell them not to worry about it—sometimes it happens to every man.

Women in most western societies have begun to understand their sexual needs more clearly. And as they became more sexually liberated after the introduction of the birth control pill and the sexual revolution in the United States of the 1970's, many women moved well beyond the "lie back and think of shopping" approach to sex. For today's modern and liberated woman, sex is no longer an unpleasant "duty" performed for the man, but it is now an enjoyable and entertaining source of pleasure for them.

This has become a jumping-off point for Female Led Relationships, and as more women began to really appreciate sex, they had to teach and control how their partners make love to them. If left unchecked, men will simply fulfill their own needs and finish way before the women could begin to start enjoying herself. In a Female Led Relationship, oral sex performed on the female pretty much becomes sex rule #1. This technique automatically slows down the man's pace and arouses the female, so she can have an orgasm and be ready for more. Trust me, men do not mind at all, they enjoy sex—any sex—and they are easily guided to pleasuring the female. I'm sure as a man you understand what I'm talking about.

Men also experience a major source of pride knowing that their women have been satisfied, hopefully reaching an orgasm multiple times. By the way, the female ability to have multiple orgasms rises in a Female Led Relationship and demonstrates to the man her sexual superiority to him. In no time at all, the man enjoys female led lovemaking over the "old-fashioned male dominated way" and is ready to become more and more obedient to the female needs as the mutual satisfaction and pleasure increases for both partners. As a man you will realize that this is a much better type of sex. So, focus on your woman's pleasure and control yourself. You will have more sex, better sex and feel happier. It is interesting, but serving women makes men happier. Most men are much happier in a Female Led Relationship than any other.

The simple request of a woman asking her man to perform oral sex is more often completely transformative. All of a sudden, men discover that racing to ejaculate is not what pleases women, and soon it will not be what pleases him either. Once males discover that females will actually enjoy lovemaking and want sex more often, even demand sex, he will be totally on board with a Female Led Relationship. You will become slower, gentler, and more aware of her needs, resulting in more intense sex. In a Female Led Relationship, much more oral sex is performed on the female than the man!

By taking the lead, women move their husbands away from a purely male perspective on sex. Women are not here to give you a blow job. Now, you are here to lick pussy. You will learn more and more about what women want and enjoy. The greatest awakening a man can experience is that, if he pleasures his

41

woman, she will be eager and demanding of more lovemaking. You will get more sex than you ever imagined.

Different women manage sex differently, but she must always be in control of the intercourse in the relationship. You must agree to this, and you must focus on her emotional, physical and psychological pleasure. It is also important to shift your focus from your sexual needs to ensure hers are satisfied. From now on, that's all that matters—her pleasure. This shift in focus entails your female to take control of your ejaculations and orgasms—complete control, which means no cheating or masturbating.

If you agree to let your Queen manage your ejaculations, I can emphasize that you will get a much better sexual experience in a Female Led Relationship. I can't explain to you how important it is for your Queen to know and feel that you really care and are truly focused on her pleasure. Most FLR men will agree that once you give up your "right" to ejaculate and orgasm, you will begin departing from your "old-fashioned, patriarchal male-dominated ways" to the new, modern female-dominated relationship.

By reading this book, you are already starting to accept your new role. You are already on your way to becoming obedient to your Queen and her needs. For many men, it starts in the bedroom and moves into the rest of the home from that point forward. Believe me, you will accept your new role because you will relax knowing you are not in charge anymore, and you don't have to act like Mr. Macho. As the relationship evolves, your ejaculation and orgasming will continue to be rewarded as a "once in a while" separate experience from an increasingly daily female-focused sexuality.

Men do not "need" to ejaculate or orgasm as often as they think, especially over the age of thirty. A *Love & Obey* Queen can often train her husband to ejaculate only with her permission and supervision. Many men have gone months at a time and say they are actually happier. The Queen can announce, "Tonight you will be allowed to orgasm because you were such a good boy..." The rest of the time, based on the Queen's desires, you will give her the oral attention she wants and, if she also wants to enjoy penetration, your hard and obedient cock will be more than ready to perform—without orgasming. Remember, you will not ejaculate all the times you penetrate the female; you simply must control yourself or be punished. As mentioned before, the focus of lovemaking is strictly on your Queen and her pleasure.

Once you realize that you are not in charge of sex and even your own penis and ejaculations, you will honestly be relieved because you will no longer experience performance anxiety. You will know that you are going to make love when your Queen desires it. In addition, because you constantly kept horny, you will be erect whenever you Queen wants to be pleasured with your penis. Since you are incredibly horny, it will not be a problem. You will also learn to love becoming the object of her desires rather than feeling that you are required to initiate sex all the time and expect the female to always be reluctant.

Now you will be freed, and you can focus on pleasing your Queen because you know that most days, she will grant you permission to ejaculate or orgasm while pleasuring her. The initial transition is often difficult and awkward, but trust me, you are a simple creature and will soon accept your woman's complete control of you and your lovemaking. The good news for you is that a sexually dominant female, who only has sex when she wants it and how she wants, will tend to be much more sexually active and the sex will become livelier and more passionate for the couple. Celebrate because now YOU WILL HAVE MORE SEX AND BETTER SEX. Although it will be DIFFERENT. In the long-term relationship, this female led lovemaking will improve your love life and the woman will be in heaven, leading to a happier more fulfilling life. Remember the old saying, "Happy wife, happy life!" It's true.

Marisa Rudder

Once you have been trained to enjoy giving in bed, it will become a behavior you will duplicate in all aspects of the relationship. For instance, you will want to clean, run errands and serve your Queen in every way possible. You will want to do these tasks to ensure your Queen is happy, and ultimately show how much you love her.

It's a Monday night and you're going to be watching a reality show instead of football. That sounds disappointing to many men. Then surprise, she wants you to go down on her, and now it's not so disappointing, is it! A casual pussy licking can work wonders for both of you. There is no pressure for you to orgasm; for now, you just want your Queen to lay back, relax, and enjoy the act of getting eaten. If your Queen orgasms, then you'll be satisfied, but don't forget to thank her when she is done, and definitely don't stop until she says stop. If it's getting you more worked up, and you want intercourse, then ask your Queen if she will allow you to service her with your penis. No matter how it ends up, a good pussy licking brings you both closer together and more in love. When your Queen orgasms, you win and it offers you a totally satisfying sensation.

This may sound strange now, but trust me, I have seen this with many couples and it is always the same outcome. Servicing the woman's pleasure becomes a more satisfying form of sex for men than they ever experienced in a patriarchal relationship. Trust me, once you embrace your Female Led Relationship, your love life will blossom. Once you become sexually obedient to your Queen, you will find that your sexuality, masculinity, and pride in your sexual prowess will be transformed to a superior level, surpassing even your own expectations of yourself as a lover. When you lose society's conventional male expectations, and follow your Queen's commands in and out of the bedroom, you both will experience a new, improved and higher level of relationship satisfaction. Female Led Relationships are more long-term and much happier than traditional man led relationships.

Of course, you want your Female Led Relationships to go well beyond the bedroom, so it's imperative that you become 100 percent obedient to your Queen in all aspects of your life together. I cannot even explain all of the huge, subtle benefits that you will both experience when committing to a loving Female Led Relationship. Too many couples pretend that they should have an equal partnership when, in fact, at home and in modern society, the female, as she has often secretly been, should be in charge.

In the past, superior women have deviously manipulated their men, but now you can be open and honest about your intent. You can explain that you are a modern "gentle" man who wants a Female Led Relationship, and you want to be obedient to your Queen because you know that in exchange for obedience, you will achieve a fulfilling and more loving life together. If you are not yet ready, keep reading. Give it a good honest amount of effort and soon you will agree that you should be in a Female Led Relationship. The following are some key points to think about in preparation of obeying and serving your Queen.

1. You always love being around your woman because she is confident.

2. You always believe her and how she often tells you the right thing to do.

3. You always want to embrace her female strength and support her ability to lead at home, at work and in society.

4. You always feel happy when you make her happy.

5. You always enjoy taking care of her and fulfilling all her needs in and out of the bedroom.

6. You experience pressure at work and in society to live up to traditional male expectations, and would like to relax and take a break from being in charge when you are at home?

7. You know she makes most of the decisions in the house anyway (with the children, etc.) so now you can just relax with it and let her take complete control.

8. You know it is easier when she tells you what she wants you to do rather than when you have to guess all the time. Imagine you will no longer have to guess what she wants, which helps take a lot of pressure off of you.

If you still are not ready to love, obey and serve your Queen after you give it all you've got, then you will have to give up on a Female Led Relationship. There are millions of men around the world (confirmed by Google search trend analysis) who are ready to love, obey and serve a strong and exciting *Love & Obey* Queen. These men quickly realize that a Female Led Relationship means that their life will be happier, calmer, more exciting, romantic and much easier if they simply accept their woman as their leader and reward her like a Queen. An obedient life to a loving female authority is life's great happiness, and if you are not going to accept that and agree to become 100 percent obedient, then you should stop reading and end your pursuit of a Female Led Relationship right now.

CHAPTER 7

> "A man must destroy every proud obstacle and all male ego that keeps him from knowing he must love and obey his woman and her many and varied desires. He must eliminate any rebellious thoughts against his Love & Obey Queen and teach his friends and sons to obey women as well. Women are simply superior and should rule over men."
>
> – Marisa Rudder

In a traditional relationship, the idea of cuckolding would not have been entertained and lumped in with cheating. But today, cuckolding is desired by many men and demanded by some Queens. Though I personally do not believe that cuckolding is necessary in a Female Led Relationship, I realize that it is something enjoyed by some couples. For some men, the act of watching their wife having sex with another man is enjoyable and some women demand it. The term cuckolding was originally a phrase used for men whose wives had sex with other men. The word itself stems from the cuckoo bird, which has a tendency to lay its eggs in another bird's nest. Recent studies show that more people are trying cuckolding as a way of spicing up the relationship. Some men feel they cannot satisfy their Queen and are open to allowing her to be with other men. Why do men like cuckolding? Some men like to watch their wives and/or girlfriends have sex with other men. They like the feeling of helplessness and being in complete submission to their woman. The turn-on is witnessing another man be sensual with your woman in front of you. Cucks may be dominant in many ways when they're alone with their woman, but when another man joins them, they become the cuck.

Typically, the Female Led Relationship-bound man will not interact with the other man; it's more about watching. Many couples claim it makes them more passionate as a couple, and most couples have certain rules they follow while they do it. If you are new to Female Led Relationships, I suggest you don't enter this arena right off the bat. Take some time to develop a strong bond with your Queen and only after some time, if you both want it, then approach it cautiously. Safety is the most important part of this type of activity and open communication is necessary. Some FLR men like the feeling of humiliation, submission and complete obedience to their woman's desires, and are exhilarated to see their wives enjoy sex with another man. Of course, some Queens demand that their husbands be okay with cuckolding because of the power she derives from being able to choose who she wants. Most couples are not into cuckolding as their Female Led Relationship involves only two people—themselves—and this is perfectly acceptable.

In our current divided political climate, the term "cuck" has become an insult for the misogynists, aimed at men they view as spineless and emasculated. The slur has its roots in the concept of cuckolding, or having an adulterous partner. Men who are feminists and support *Love & Obey* Queenship understand that cuckolding is acceptable—although not right for everyone. Naturally, you will be criticized by misogynist men if you support women having cuckolding, but in the female led community, the main rule is that the man supports the Queen's desires. Women know that many men secretly desire their women experiencing cuckolding, and there is nothing wrong with it as long as your Queen works out the details with you as her primary man (husband or boyfriend). Once boundaries and rules are established, women can fulfill this fantasy in many different ways. And here is news for ignorant misogynist men—according to a recent study, acting on threesomes, cuckolding or group sex fantasies can be a largely positive experience for many couples, and hardly a sign of male weakness. So, if you and your Queen desire it, ignore the misogynist critics and enjoy yourselves.

References to cuckolding appear in literature as early as the 13th century, usually in the form of male characters who fear that their child has been sired by another man during an act of infidelity. However, today cuckolding has become fetishized into a powerful sexual fantasy for many men who get aroused by the idea of their romantic partner engaging in sexual activity with someone else. Women also share this fantasy and once you have agreed to a Female Led Relationship, the woman knows she is in control and can do what she desires and you must accept it and obey her desires. This fantasy has been around as long as marriage and sexuality itself. Today, threesomes, cuckolding or group sex in heterosexual couples is becoming increasingly popular, and more people are rejecting the social misogynist stigma against these fantasies. A survey of thousands of Americans found that 93 percent of men and about 66 percent of women have fantasized about threesomes, cuckolding or group sex.

Usually, men are more likely to fantasize about cuckolding, but there are a number of women who have these fantasies as well, which points to the need for more research focused on women's cuckolding desires. Remember, in a Female Led Relationship, sex is for the woman's pleasure. The man's pleasure comes from bringing the female sexual gratification. So, if the female desires more men, then the man should oblige and be happy for her to be pleasured as she wishes. In a Female Led

Relationship the sexual goddess within a woman will be released and this emerging sex goddess will be supported by the man. The man enjoys his submissive servant role to his sexually superior woman. He also likes being involved in a type of relationship that is considered by many misogynist men as taboo. The *Love & Obey* man becomes a sexual gourmet and he learns to savor the taste of exotic taboo female led intimacies. He even enjoys the extreme fantasies of interracial and BDSM themes in his cuckolding experience. Naturally, the motivations behind what makes cuckolding arousing in male fantasies will be different from man to man. But what makes cuckolding arousing for most men is that they tend to view it as a taboo act. In a patriarchal society or culture that idealizes monogamy, the cuckold fantasy is a current narrative that is available for certain people to conceptualize their sexual fantasies and rebel against the norm.

As a relationship expert, one of the more intriguing findings from my study of the impact of cuckolding on Female Led Relationships is that it adds to the female role as the sexually dominant leader and makes the man accept even her most extreme desires. Even cuckolding, threesomes or group sex with other men are viewed as part of her sexual superiority. Overall, I have found that for the most part, cuckolding tends to be a positive experience in the female led lifestyle. There doesn't appear to be evidence of a disturbance to the women's control or disrespect for one's male partner. With that said, cuckolding, threesomes and other sexual behavior can successfully be added to the FLR if conducted in a responsible and respectful manner.

The Queen should consider the male partner because men in female led relationships often have a fear of losing their Queen's love and being abandoned. This can cause men extreme anxiety. However, once a man becomes confident that this will not be the case, the Queen can proceed with her chosen extra-sexual activities. I have found that certain personality factors do predict more positive experiences when a Queen decides to act on cuckolding fantasies. Men who undergo relationship anxiety or abandonment issues, who lack proper intimacy and communication with their Queen, and whose Queen isn't a careful, detail-oriented planner, then acting on a consensual non-monogamous fantasy can very quickly turn into an extremely negative experience.

In other words, the Queen has to clearly explain what she is planning. Here are my suggestions:

1. Ask your Queen to explain the scenario she desires with you and explain what she desires and be specific about what she is going to do.

   (a) Does she want to have sex with another man and you together, or does she want you to watch? Or does she want to have sex alone while you wait at home and clean the house?

   (b) Does she want to have the other man to only perform oral sex on her and only allow you to have intercourse with her, or vice-versa?

   (c) Together, you should agree on the boundaries that could change. Sometimes at first, the Queen will agree to get you adjusted by simply allowing the other man to perform oral sex on her the first time. Once you, the husband or boyfriend, gets used to that experience, she will then add having intercourse. This gradual approach—one step at a time can be a good way to enjoy expanding your sex life without any negative impact.

2. Ask your Queen to explain why she is doing it.

   (a) We know that women, more than men, tend to feel stifled and bored by long-term exclusivity—despite having been misled that they were designed for monogamy. Many women think they want monogamy. It's a cozy arrangement, and one our culture endorses, to put it mildly. However, biologically and in a primitive natural environment, human and female animals have sex with many men to continue the species and often many men are allowed to attempt fertilization of female humans. Similar to male animals to female animals in the wild. So, it's understandable that wanting monogamy isn't the same as feeling a natural, biological, sexual desire in a long-term monogamous partnership. Moving in with your boyfriend can kill your sex drive, as much as a married lifestyle can.

3. Ask your Queen to explain if she is criticizing you as her lover, even if you give her lots of orgasms, or does she view you as inadequate?

    (a) Remember, women in a Female Led Relationship will by design become more selfish and entitled, as well as very savvy sexual strategists. They will learn how to manipulate you to get what they want because they know this is what you will want her to do. Studies have shown that women living with a partner in a man-led relationship were more likely to lack interest in sex. A Finnish seven-year study of more than 2,100 women revealed that women in the same man-led relationship reported less desire, arousal and satisfaction.

    (b) Ask your Queen to explain why you, as her husband or boyfriend, should be happy that she will be enjoying some extra pleasure. Most men in patriarchal society complain that women have a lower libido or sexual desire level than their male partners after a year or more of marriage, and in the longer term as well. The complaint has historically been attributed to that lower baseline libido for women, but that explanation conveniently ignores how women regularly start relationships equally as excited for sex as men. Remember the honeymoon stage. Women in long-term, committed heterosexual partnerships have been brainwashed to think they don't want sex because they naturally have a lower sexual desire level than their husbands, but that's not the case. The truth is that they've lost interest in the predictable sex with the same person over and over.

(c) In reality, they simply need more for their sexual arousal and excitement. Remember, in a Female Led Relationship, women are freed and allowed to rule as they see fit. Their inner sexual goddess is set free. So, in many ways it is natural for a woman in an FLR to desire additional partners and more sexual variations. Despite the common patriarchal view, women like desire and need more sex than men do to be happy and satisfied.

Despite the fact that women are more sexual than men, not every couple who has a threesome, cuckolding or group sex fantasy should think about acting on it. As I mentioned above, you need to be very clear with each other about the limits and each of your roles in these extra sexual activities. For example, the other man is only allowed to perform oral sex in the beginning, then add intercourse later. Or perhaps only you are allowed to perform oral sex on her, or you are only allowed to watch. You need to be clear on the rules, each other's boundaries and expectations because the emotions from seeing your partner with someone else can be a turn-on or be a shocking blow. Especially in a real cuckolding experience, there needs to be an element of humiliation, degradation or denial. The woman has to be elevated to a sexually superior status and the men have to be demoted to a less than adequate status to satisfy her. Even though our erotic imaginations have the ability to turn "shameful" lemons into "delicious kink" lemonade, you need to proceed with caution and care in these extra sexual activities to ensure a successful, positive experience for you as a couple.

Fantasies about voyeurism seem to overlap with those regarding threesomes, cuckolding or group sex in most men. It's a forbidden sexual desire that can be easily customized to meet a wide range of sexual needs and desires for their *Love & Obey* Queen, whether it's taboo sex, novelty, voyeurism or something else. Men will enjoy fantasizing about the idea of his superior Queen having a threesome with another man or enjoying group sex with men.

Remember that acting on these fantasies is very powerful stuff, and sometimes just sharing a sexy thought can be arousing enough—you don't have to follow through. If you are thinking about acting on a threesome, cuckolding or group sex fantasy, it's worth stepping back first and making sure your relationship is in a good place and that you have strong sexual communication skills.

For men and couples considering the issue of threesomes, cuckolding or group sex, it's important that you both be honest, act with integrity, communicate clearly, and understand and share the same sexual values. I've seen men who try to trick their wives into threesomes, cuckolding or group sex, and this never ends up well. That said, the rewards can be amazing, I have spoken with many female led couples and they have told me about their success of adding a threesome, cuckold and group sex play into their relationships in a positive way.

For couples who do decide to move forward, it's important to take things slow. The reality of watching your spouse have sex with someone else—or knowing they're doing it if you're not there—is often very different than the fantasy expectations. The outcome can dredge up powerful emotions, so take baby steps and keep communicating with each other. Remember, in a liberated female led world, women cannot be stereotyped, pigeonholed or limited in what they want or do; the glory of human sexuality is its variation and flexibility. So, when women speak of desire in the future, we should acknowledge that the superior sex thirsts for the excitement of an encounter with someone or something new as much as (really more) than men do—and that they could benefit from a hall pass to try it out.

CHAPTER 8

> "Today women are becoming enlightened. More women realize that husbands should submit to them in order to achieve a happier life. Even though the Bible doesn't say so. It is true in the modern world and couples are realizing it now more than ever."
>
> – Marisa Rudder

Unfortunately, not all women realize their natural superiority to men and they need to be enlightened. In this chapter, I will share some of my secret tips regarding if you want an FLR but your woman is reluctant or you don't have a dominant woman yet. What if you are reading this book and your woman is submissive, or you don't even have any woman? Suppose you want to find a dominant woman, or you want your woman to rise up to become your Queen and take control of your relationship. How do you get her to change into your Queen? It's not as difficult as you might think to find dominant women or release the Queen inside the woman you already have.

Most men, especially those who work at an executive or management level, are used to acting in a leadership role both at work and at home. Most men are used to sitting at the head of the table, in the driver's seat, and controlling the TV remote control. Men are trained and conditioned by society that they need to be in charge and make all the decisions and call the shots.

There is no doubt that men have enjoyed this power and control in the past. But it is exhausting, and deep down inside many men crave a chance to relax from all the pressure of being a man in the old patriarchal society. You desire a vacation from having the weight of the world on your shoulders. You need a world where your woman takes charge and you can simply sit back, relax and experience what it is like to be in the passenger's seat. You want to experience someone else being in charge and responsible for the decision-making and you just want to do what you are told in a relaxing and calm way. You secretly want this from your woman. More specifically, you often want your girlfriend or wife to take charge of your relationship so that you can have a break from it all.

The problem arises because many women are also programmed by society to appear to be the submissive type because they grew up with those old-fashioned beliefs and were trained that way. Many women have never had any experience making decisions or calling the shots. Many women are even uncomfortable having sex with a man when they are on top. Millions of men struggle with this problem and even struggle with the simple decision to tell their women about their secret desire for a Female Led Relationship. What usually tips the scales and gets the man to breakdown is they find themselves fantasizing about a strong confident woman being in charge of them way too often, and they want to find a way to turn their fantasy into reality. Eventually just looking at erotic photos and videos of female domination is not enough. At some point you want your woman to take control and dominate you in a loving way.

You can find a dominant woman, or turn your submissive woman into a dominant woman, if you follow the steps in this book and become a gentleman. When you demonstrate gentlemanly behavior in society and show respect and support to women in society, dominant women will notice. They will see that you are a good man and can love, obey and serve her well. Society is better to use "language that is generally accepted in society" rather than FemDom or BDSM language. Don't tell "vanilla" women, even if they are strong powerful women in society, that you fantasize about them wearing black leather outfits and whipping you in a dungeon until you are very deep in a relationship, and expect that they will understand your fantasy. Most women will be immediately turned off by this approach. Instead, try a smoother, gentler approach to get the message across that you are looking for a woman that you can LOVE, OBEY and SERVE. Understand we are a new movement that is growing but not yet universally accepted. You have to bring many women over to the female led lifestyle slowly and gradually.

Tell "vanilla" albeit powerful women in society that you love strong, educated, dynamic, powerful women who know what they want and how to get it. Tell women that you respect them and think they are absolutely amazing. Tell them you are impressed with their degrees, careers and other accomplishments. Let them know that you are good with a modern liberated woman who lives life on her terms. Once you have praised them, let them know that you view yourself as a "complete and total GENTLEMAN"; that you believe in the **OLD SCHOOL CHIVALRY,** and you believe men should be brave, courteous, honorable and gallant toward women. Tell them you are old-fashioned in that way and enjoy being in the service of women, but yet you are also modern because dislike misogynists, patriarchal thinking men, and that you are a man-feminist as well. Tell them that you often think of yourself as a modern day "knight in shining armor" who recognizes that modern women are just as intelligent, strong and capable as any many out secretly believe that women are even superior to men in many ways. It's also good to mention that you like doing things around the house and that you believe men should carry their load of household and child rearing chores right alongside of women.

Once you get started in your new lifestyle, whether it is with a new woman or a woman you are already involved with, you may feel the thrilling effect of your secret female domination fantasy and be tempted to move fast in your relationship. You might become frustrated, withdrawn, and lose some of your connection with your woman, but this is commonly experienced when a couple starts feeling more like roommates than romantic partners. You must be patient and move in the direction you desire slowly and carefully.

What really scares men is when they finally realize that the longer they go without a dominant female figure in their life and the more they try to repress the idea of a Queen being in control, the more the desire for an FLR grows in their hearts. Finally, most men realize deep down that they cannot continue living a patriarchal lie, which gives men the courage to reveal their desires for a Female Led Relationship. When men finally bring up the idea, especially to women who view themselves as "vanilla" or traditionally feminine and submissive, the woman's response is almost always negative.

They are not necessarily angry or upset, but they are confused and usually when a person is perplexed, they will say no to a new idea. When an unfamiliar and confusing idea enters a relationship, it leads to a number of questions and potential problems in communication. It's okay. I will guide you through the relationship minefield and get you safely to a Female Led Relationship.

Many women in a relationship will initially be thinking, "Is my man, so unhappy with the way things are that he is looking for something new and different? Is there something wrong with me because I can't open up to new ideas? Are we no longer compatible, and are we headed for a break up? Your woman may experience a number of serious questions and a high-level confusion, leading her to say "no" but do not despair, there is a way to release her inner Queen.

A Female Led Relationship can be strange for people who grew up in traditional households where the father occupied the head of the household role, while the mother occupied the caretaker and supportive housekeeper role, faithfully fulfilling all her duties as a good wife and mother. One reason Female Led Relationships are exploding in society and becoming the new norm is due to how many men are raised in a single mother household. A whole generation of young men have now grown up with absent fathers and they are already accustomed to and prefer the loving female authority of their single mother. Mother, stepmom and MILF fantasizes are very common in men.

So, the new model of the MOTHER being in charge of the house and being in charge of teaching and raising young men is becoming very normal. Still, for some men and women raised in traditional households in which the mother cooks, cleans and raises the kids while the father is the head of household breadwinner, it can be challenging to flip the script and change roles. Many men and women just don't know what to make of it. The very thought of it, seems a bit...unnatural, and more importantly, when the traditionally conditioned female mind tries to imagine a female led home, they find it doesn't have much appeal.

Often couples with this problem reach a gridlock much like rush hour traffic on the freeway. They are simply going nowhere fast. For many couples, it seems like each partner has conflicting desires and neither one of them are able to conceive what to do about it. So, they each revert back to their secret or traditional way of living, with a slim hope that something will suddenly change but it never does. Luck won't change outcomes and that's why I am writing this section in my book.

I want to offer some guidance to people who are stuck in a cross-thinking-traffic-jam. I wanted to reach out to people in this frustrating situation, and see what I can do to change it for the better. I am sharing my thoughts, and I'm going to explain some simple principles to you. First, relationships flow between each partner and their needs and desires can evolve. Even if one person in the relationship is against a change, there are ways you can make her change. Leadership, power and control in a relationship can move from the man to the woman and the relationship dynamics can change, so there is hope for you.

Here's how you can start to change your relationship from man led to female led. First, if you are the man, you will need to start acting more helpful to your woman and start doing chores (dishes, vacuuming, laundry, etc.) around your house. Tell her that you think she is working too hard and you want to help. She will appreciate you and start to see glimpses of a new path. Second, you will need to start acting more submissive and more like a "gentle" man; let her choose movies, TV shows and where you go out to eat. When you have an argument, tell her you realize that she is right and you apologize for arguing with her. Inform her she looks tired from being on her feet all day, and you want to give her a foot massage. When she offers to give you a blow job, suggest you will reciprocate and give her oral too.

Naturally, she will start to subconsciously shift into the opposite role that you are taking on. She will start to choose the movies and restaurants. She will start to expect that you clean up around the house. She will expect to win arguments. She will expect you to reciprocate and perform oral sex on her when she performs it on you. Casually, tell her from time to time at the right moment that she reminds you of a Queen or a Goddess. Now my friend, the process will begin and soon she will begin to direct in more ways as you begin to follow her lead.

Now, let me pause before you think I am trying to tell you to manipulate your woman. It is not about manipulation; it is about seduction. You need to seduce the deeper parts of her womanhood, and believe me, all women have this inside of themselves. You need to release her inner Goddess and her inner Queen. It's about genuinely using your skills in a way that will mentally and emotionally appeal to her in an unexpected way. It's about behaving in a specific way that will please your wife in mysterious ways she has never experienced before, and these new experiences in your relationship will start to become irresistibly attractive. She will want you to do more chores. Let her choose which activities you do together. Compliment her more often. Perform oral sex on her more often. This is the simplest and fastest way that will naturally convert your partner into subconsciously desiring a dominant role. You simply help your partner make a mental, emotional and pleasurable connection to this way of life without ever mentioning terms like Female Led Relationship, Queen or man slave. This is a subtle love and obey teaching technique that works. This way of seduction is much more effective than trying to blurt out that you want to live a Female Led Relationship when your partner probably doesn't even know what you're talking about.

Start slow, be patient and win her over step-by-step. In no time at all she'll be wearing leather, bossing you around and demanding that you go down on her. Once she starts to warm up to your subtle seduction, you can reveal that your friend read an interesting book and gave it to you, which you found fascinating. It's called *Love & Obey* and you can give it to your woman. This will start to make all the terminology and fantasies into a reality for her. She will soon be your Queen!

However, at first your partner needs to be able to make a gradual mental and emotional connection to the female led experience in order to be willing to explore it. The way you present your lifestyle change to her is the most important factor in determining whether or not she'll be able to connect with it. Knowing what, when, where and how to express the right ideas can be extremely complex because a small mistake can set you back or even ruin your chances. You need to present new ideas in a way that turns your partner on and not off. You do not want your partner to wonder who you have become or to lose respect for you. More importantly, you need to present it in a way that will inspire your partner to open up. Often times when we think we know what will inspire our partner, we are proven wrong because our desires cloud our thinking. We confuse our wants to what would inspire women to open up.

HERE IS ONE GIANT LOVE & OBEY SECRET THAT REALLY WORKS!

Remember back to the time when you first fell in love with each other, or first started dating. You wanted to do everything to win her over. You wanted to build and strengthen the intimacy and connection you shared. You wanted her to fall in love with you. Changing the way a woman feels about leading in a relationship, or a man feels about being obedient, can seriously impact a partner's feelings for you in a negative way if you are not careful. Fortunately, though, you don't have to go through these changes alone; I am here to help you. So, start remembering how you behaved when you were first dating and start getting into that "courting" role again. Over the last twenty-five years, I have been studying, learning and professionally helping people to navigate their personal mental and physical barriers to Female Led Relationships and I know how to make it a successful transition.

Here are some simple steps that trigger effective psychological and emotional responses with her that will help her to accept that you are now living to please and service her. Start slow and before you know it, you'll begin to see your relationship dynamic transform right before your very eyes. Men, if you want your woman to act like a Queen, you have to start rewarding her like a Queen.

Practical and simple steps to take:

1. Rub her feet with lotion.

2. Offer to run a bath for her.

3. Assist her around the house and start doing the laundry, clean the kitchen, bathroom and wash the dishes.

4. Bring her a cup of coffee and breakfast in bed on the weekend.

5. Give her a full body massage, and when the timing feels right, ask her if you can try something a little different and go down on her until she orgasms. Stop after she orgasms and tell her how much you enjoyed that experience. When she asks about you and your erection, play it cool and tell her don't worry about me. I just wanted to give you a reward tonight. This will start to transfer the sex act from something she has to do as her "wifely" duty to something that she wants to do because she is going to experience great pleasure from it.

6. Let her watch what she wants on TV, or let her choose which movie to go see or which restaurant she wants to dine in on Friday night.

7. In general, ask her if there is anything you can do for her. Always act like a gentleman: open her car door, pull out her chair in the restaurant, give her your coat when it's cold out, etc.

8. As she starts to become more demanding of you sexually and otherwise, thank her for giving you the opportunity to make her happy. Also tell her how much you love her and doing things for her. As you progress and she starts to take the lead, share with her that you love her more than ever now.

9. One last tip. She wants a really good kisser, and she will probably get super hyped about you also being good at oral. However, being a good kisser in and of itself shouldn't be taken for granted. Study the kiss. If you're not good at performing oral, study going down on her. You need to know how to work your tongue in both situations. She will appreciate you for the orgasms as well as the passionate kisses you give her, too. So, men practice and learn how to use your mouth. Trust me, the tongue is mightier than the penis. Learn to go down and kiss well.

Hopefully, you are getting the idea. Stop being a typical selfish "old school" man and start thinking of the many ways you can pamper your wife. Try doing one thing each day. She will probably wonder what has gotten into you but don't stop. Just tell her that you realize how much she means to you, how happy she makes you, and you just want to show your appreciation. Tell her she is your life and making her happy means everything to her. Eventually, at moments when she takes charge—tell her you worship her. REAL MEN WORSHIP WOMEN. Once your wife starts to get a taste of what it is like to be pampered, she will start to enjoy it and crave more. So, keep it up and step it up to higher and higher levels.

When you do these special things for her on a daily basis, and you start to act more like an obedient gentleman, then you can politely ask her to start acting differently too. Tell her that you get in the mood doing what you do when she also does things a certain way, and this seduction can definitely start in the bedroom.

1. Put out some candles on the dinner table and make your newly rising Queen her favorite food (but not dessert). Come out in some cool clothes that turn her on and if you don't have any, go buy some.

2. After that romantic dinner, let her know you feel frisky, and you want her for dessert. Pleasure her right there at the table or take her to the bedroom and go down her— she'll love how you are spicing things up. She'll also learn to set romantic candle light dinners because she will want to be your dessert again and again. She'll become more of a seductress.

3. Wherever you do it, tantalizingly start licking, kissing and sucking her clit and pussy with a confident, mischievous look in your eyes and bring her to an orgasm, and only stop when she says she can't take it anymore. Then inform her that you're turned on by her being in control.

4. Ask her to tie you up to the bed, and while you are lying on your back, have her place her pussy on your face and start grinding it against your mouth and nose until she cums all over your face. And don't stop there; ask her to climb on top of you and to ride you. When you feel like she is starting to cum, say to her how much you love her being a woman on top and ask if she is okay with that.

5. When you are making love to her, tell her you like serving her pussy and serving her every whim. Do this before, during, and after your lovemaking sessions. Tell her you really hope she is okay with her being pleasured like this in your sex life because it really turns you on. Ask her if she has enjoyed your new philosophy on lovemaking and being a gentleman to her.

6. Randomly grab her and then lead her to the bedroom, telling her, "When you're in charge of me, it puts me in the mood."

7. Ask her again if she enjoys your new ways.

8. Tell her that you're not sure what has come over you, but you think that so much more is possible...if she will only let you serve her in your sex life.

9. Eventually start to let her know your preference for her to continue fulfilling her new leadership role in your relationship, if she doesn't mind. In a flirting way, tell her that it will definitely be worth her while.

10. Finally, after this has become acceptable to her, introduce my book *Love & Obey* to her and reveal your desire to start living a Female Led Relationship because you know it will make you both happier and closer than ever before.

After you have been implementing this new lifestyle slowly and gradually over a few months, she will realize that life and your relationship has become so much better. She will then be open to becoming your full-time Queen, as you have shown her the benefits of enjoying a gentleman's obedient service.

After a month or a couple of months (results vary from woman to woman) of your great, new approach to your relationship and sex life, let your woman know that you want her to become much more dominant in your sex life and your daily relations. Let her know that she is now your Goddess or Queen. From time to time, start calling her by your/her favorite name until you use it almost always. Most modern couples think that they should be balanced or equal partners. This doesn't really maximize a relationship for either partner. Deep down you need to bring out her desire to be a dominant loving *Love & Obey* Queen. Reassure her that you think it takes a real man to serve a real woman like her, and that you want her to be your Queen while you will be her knight in shining armor. Let her know that the BEST THING she ever did was take charge in the bedroom. Hands down. Let her know that not only are you enjoying making love to her more than ever, but you enjoy being more thoughtful, accommodating and obedient to her in and out of the bedroom. Ask her if she enjoys being in charge while you are her thoughtful gentleman. Tell her you just love it and you hope she does too!

Listen guys, I don't need to tell you every detail but she will take charge and run your relationship once you allow her control of your sexuality. For example, take action on what I've mentioned above on a weekly/daily basis. When you're in bed with your woman and she is still sleeping, wake her up to the soft caress of your tongue on her pussy. When she opens her eyes and turns toward you, look at her with a spark in your eye and give a devious smile.

"I love you so much," you tell her, as you let her orgasm in your mouth, and then thank her for letting you taste her cum. Tell her you love her being in charge and you love obeying and serving her every time you make her cum. This will make her associate dominating and leading you with a pleasurable act. Tell her you will love her more and do anything in the world for her at that moment right after her orgasm.

You know the rest of it guys, just do what you like to do and make sure she orgasms. When she is done, tell her she is now officially in a Female Led Relationship. Let her know that you believe you have both just seriously changed your relationship for the better with this new way of living. Thank her for being open-minded and taking charge. Then finally disclose that this lifestyle is way more manly and that she has become a complete Goddess to you.

A Female Led Relationship creates real intimacy between a woman and a man, so your woman will be open to your desires and what you want to explore, and if right, your woman will actually crave more leadership and more obedience from you.

You will both learn that almost everything we have learned about women, sex and relationships are wrong. Now you can use your new Female Led Relationship to find "happily ever after." Just use your head and give head in your foreplay to turn her on more than she has ever been turned on. Tell her that if she keeps up this new empowered female behavior, you'll be getting better and better at being obedient and serving her ever need as your great and powerful Queen.

Simply set the stage and you will get your partner begging you to go deeper and deeper into a Female Led Relationship. The secret is praising your partner for acting the way you desire. For you, tell her you will always love, obey and serve her as a gentleman. For her, tell her you love her as your Queen or Goddess and you want her to feel new confident and enjoy her new take charge style. These compliments will actually elevate and inspire you both to get more involved in the female led lifestyle. Any woman can be transformed from meek and mild to a dominant Queen in and out of the bedroom. Any man can be trained to be obedient and more gentlemanly and to love, obey and serve. A Female Led Relationship will quickly go from a suggestion and an idea, into something you and your partner take completely seriously and live up on a daily basis. Once you unleash the Queen inside her, and the gentleman inside you, you will both discover a world unlike any other.

It is up to you as a couple to determine exactly what kind of FLR you want to enjoy. It can be an extreme BDSM, a sexually open, or a milder monogamous lifestyle. It is up to you to structure your relationship dynamic the way you want it to be, whether it's limited, or covers every area of your life. Or usually something in between the extremes. It's up to the two of you, and I don't know what you both desire, or can handle, so it's ultimately a very personal choice in the end. Only you know yourselves. I am giving you a guide; you can work out the details of how you make a healthy, happy Female Led Relationship that you and your partner will both enjoy for years to come.

There is just one basic rule. The woman rules and the man obeys. If you are married, I want to teach each one of you to love your wife more than yourself, and to show your wife that you respect her above all else. If you are single, I want you to find a woman to love, obey and serve—introduce yourself as a gentleman and tell her you are looking for your Queen. Most women can handle that. I have also made it easy for you. After you set the groundwork, let her read your copies of *Love & Obey* and *Real Men Worship Women*. My books will add the final touches on all of your preparation as your new woman and relationship make the switch into female led mode.

CHAPTER 9

"A man must endure any persecution and ridicule from old school patriarchal, misogynistic men patiently, obeying his woman's commands and maintaining his belief in her as his loving female authority."

– Marisa Rudder

Now let's go back to the most important rule of them all— be obedient! The role of obedience in relationships is key to creating a hierarchy of power. Obedience is a form of social influence in which an individual acts in response to a direct order from another individual, who is usually an authority figure. It is assumed that without such an order, the person would not have acted in any particular way. Following commands is an essential requirement in a Female Led Relationship. A command given by the *Love & Obey* Queen to the gentleman is a demand for them to follow it without thinking or disobeying.

This is important because orders instill discipline. Orders are passed from the Queen to the submissive man, as a way of ensuring they are both on the same page. Obedience is the following of orders and plays the role of maintaining structure in the Female Led Relationship. Leadership entails commanding respect and a predictable response from the obedient man. Queens have to demonstrate that they have the capacity to lead others, and they show this by their ability to successfully complete tasks. For example, graduating from high school, college, graduate school, or as a professional working successfully in a career. To be a *Love & Obey* Queen, a woman should demonstrate that she can run, manage and maintain order in your relationship. As I mentioned earlier, most women who desire FLR are well-educated and smart. Often, they are better educated and smarter than their man, so this is not usually an issue.

Obedience is nothing new in society and in our interpersonal relationships. So, it's not surprising that it plays a key role in a Female Led Relationship. Many traditional cultures regard obedience as a virtue. Historically, societies have expected children to obey their elders. Think about it, throughout time; in colonial America slaves to their owners, in feudal society serfs to their lords and lords to their king, and everyone to God. Compare the religious ideal of surrender and its importance in Islam, the word Islam literally means "surrender." In some Christian weddings, obedience is formally included along with honor and love as part of a conventional bride's, but not the bridegroom's wedding vow. In a Female Led Relationship, it is the opposite, the man vows obedience but the *Love & Obey* Queen only promises to lead and command. As a man you must obey your superior woman, calling her Goddess or Queen. You should behave as obedient as a child does with his mother, and if you do good, you will not have to fear any frightening punishment. Whatever your woman says to you, do as she tells you, for through her, you will win her love and achieve happiness.

Obedience is required when you are told to do something by the female authority figure. Whereas traditional man-female roles are determined by conformity to social pressures and adhering to the norms of the majority. Obedience involves a hierarchy of power and status. The person giving the order, Queen, has a higher status in the relationship than the person receiving the order, the obedient gentleman. This higher status creates order, calm and creates a nurturing loving environment.

Obedience is the act of following orders without question because they come from an authority that you have accepted. There are many legitimate authorities in a person's life, from parents to teachers to law enforcement, and even spiritual and government leaders. Most of these authority figures mentioned above were given their authority by society. We are just told to follow what they tell you to do. In other words, we are trained to be obedient to these people. Every person at some time in their life has followed a superior without questioning why they are doing what they are doing. For example, we never question why we take tests in school. We just take them because we are told to do so. We never question a lot of the rules that people say "are in our best interest" because they are usually told to us by someone who is in a position higher than us. In the Female Led Relationship, the woman is granted the highest position of authority, and the man agrees to obey her. In exchange, he earns the right to live in a safe, loving and compassionate female led lifestyle.

Chaos is a situation of confusion, a disorderly state, and lacking leadership. With an accepted authority figure and strict obedience, any guesswork on what to do goes away, and reduces anxiety on how to respond in various situations. Loving female authority gives her control over you and also expects your obedience. Her orders and your obedience determine the positions of power that defines the role of you and your woman. Once you accept your woman as your Queen, and she accepts you as her obedient gentleman, you will see that you have eliminated elements of a presumption and incidents of confusion.

Additionally, orders establish a control of various situations. Hearing your Queen commands, you take action immediately and follow her orders. This behavior pattern eliminates instances of second-guessing, wrong decisions, fear, and failure to follow her preferred course of action. This predictable behavior pattern also helps prevent any breakdown in communication and the relationship. Following your female's commands upholds the chain of authority. In every human institution, individuals follow a particular existing hierarchy, from the superiors to the junior staff. In the military, for instance, the chain of command defines its leadership system. In the military, everyone has a rank and there is a chain of command. Within corporations, people have positions and jobs, from the lowest with no authority to the highest person who is in charge of the corporations' plan of action. It is the same in a Female Led Relationship.

The failure to follow orders appears as disrespect to the *Love & Obey* Queen, which is an offense that requires punishment. The Queen may not necessarily ask or give a clear order, but the submissive man is obliged nevertheless to obey. Moreover, since the obedient man takes a command before beginning any task, he promises to uphold the desires of the female through showing allegiance to her as his rightful leader and following her orders. The Female Led Relationship structure emphasizes the values and principles of discipline and respect for the Queen's absolute authority. To portray these values, gentlemen have to obey and follow orders given, as they work towards achieving the female's life goals. Only with your obedience can you maintain a loving Female Led Relationship.

CHAPTER 10

> "A man must obey his Love & Obey Queen, and do what she says. A woman's work is to watch over her man, and as a woman, you are accountable for his care. A man must give his woman a reason to love him with joy and not with pain. That would certainly not be in a man's best interest."
>
> – Marisa Rudder

Note: *As I mentioned in the beginning, because your woman is in charge, there are some parts of this book you should share with her. This chapter is designed for use by you and your Queen together. You should ask her to read it along with you and start to implement some of these effective audio-visual teaching techniques. If you don't have a woman yet, or your woman has not accepted her role as your Queen, you can just read this chapter by yourself and share it later.*

Audio visual teaching is an audio-visual teaching method that uses a simple stimulus (a sound or gesture) that Psychologists refer to as operant conditioning. The system uses audio and/or visual conditioning reinforcers, which a Queen can deliver quickly and precisely instead of a primary reinforcer, such as a food reward like a cookie. Or maybe she will tell you that she allows you to buy some new tools or sporting equipment that you want, if he behaves properly.

The term "audio teaching" comes from using a specific word and inflection spoken by the trainer that precisely marks the desired behavior. When teaching a new behavior, the audio cue helps the man to quickly identify the precise behavior that will result in a reward or punishment for him at a later time. The technique is very convenient because it can be used discreetly in public locations without having to reveal you are in a Female Led Relationship. This matters to some people who like to keep the nature of their relationship private.

Sometimes, instead of a verbal cue or a spoken word like "bravo" to mark the desired behavior, other distinctive sounds can be made. You can "whistle, cluck your tongue, or snap your fingers" or even use a visual signal, such as a hand sign or sign language as necessary with hard of hearing or deaf men. The reason why the audio-visual teaching method is useful is because it can be implemented anywhere and at any time promptly and precisely to create the required mental connections for speedy learning. The first step in audio visual teaching is instructing the man to associate the sound (which I mentioned earlier can be a word, whistle, cluck of your tongue, or snap of your fingers) or a visual signal (high five, thumbs up or sign language) with a reward that he will receive at a later time and place. Every time the audio cue or visual signal is given, a reward must be delivered by the Queen for doing something that pleased her.

The Queen's audio cue or visual signal is used to let the man know that she is happy with a desired behavior. Most women already do this naturally by giving a man "the look" when he does something displeasing or a "warm smile" when he does something pleasing. In fact, audio visual teaching can be as simple as using "the look" and the "warm smile" to train your man and then let him know later that he is getting this reward because of what he did when you gave him the "warm smile." Or he is getting a "time out" or "TV privileges" taken away because of what he did when you gave him "the look." In this audio-visual teaching, you will officially explain what everything means and what will happen to him when he acts good or bad. The following are some ways how you can use this cue or signal:

1. **Catching**: the man in the act of doing something that is desired, for example preparing you a coffee or tea, or running your bath. Eventually the man learns to repeat the behavior because he knows he will get a reward.

2. **Shaping:** gradually building a new behavior by rewarding each small step.

3. **Luring:** using the reward like a magnet to get the man to ask for the desired action so the Queen says what she wants. If you would like tickets to the football game, well, you must do something for me!

You will need to let your man know exactly what the audio cue or visual signal for the behavior is, such as a word like "attaboy" or a hand signal like a "thumbs up." The man will learn a reward is on the way after completing the desired behavior once he sees or hears a signal from you. This will become your secret communication together. When he hears your audio cue or sees your visual signal, he will get excited because he knows he will be rewarded. I personally like "snapping my fingers." My man instantly knows he has misbehaved and that I am annoyed. The basis of effective audio-visual teaching is precise timing to deliver the conditioned reinforcer at the same moment as the desired behavior is acted out. The cue or signal is used as a bridge between the marking of a good behavior when it happens, and the rewarding with a primary reinforcer such as "tickets to the game" or a "blow job."

The behavior can be elicited by **LURING** in which a hand gesture or a sound is used to coax the man to do something for you. **SHAPING** can be used when your man's behavior gets closer to the desired behavior and you give him an "Attaboy!"

CAPTURING can be used when the man's spontaneous offering of a desired behavior is rewarded. Once a behavior is learnt, you will simply be able to give your man a signal of what you want him to do and he will do it instinctively because he has been trained that this is a good behavior and that it will result in a reward.

Audio and visual teaches wanted behaviors by rewarding actions when they happen, and it does not use punishment, which is a big positive for me. I don't use the whole BDSM/FEMDOM corporal punishment scene. I prefer positive reinforcement to maintain discipline in a loving FLR. I believe it enhances a positive lifestyle full of love and romance.

Audio visual teaching uses almost entirely positive reinforcements. Some audio-visual teaching can use mild corrections such as a "non-reward marker" like "ughhh!" or a sigh like "ohhh!" to let your man know that the behavior is not correct. Or a correction, such as a "time out" in which attention is removed from the man and he must sit quietly and reflect on his bad behavior.

None of this teaching is mean or intense, and it may seem silly to some, but it establishes the female's authority in the relationship. It reinforces that the woman is in charge and that the man must obey what she says and seek approval on all his actions. This teaching is actually very mild in appearance but powerful in its psychological impact because it will signal to him that you are the boss and he must do as he is told. Eventually, this teaching will fade out from the obvious and formal way it starts in the beginning and becomes part of your natural interaction. He will know when he gets "the look" or you "snap your fingers" that you are displeased. Or if he hears "attaboy!" and sees a "warm smile," he knows he's behaving well. If he doesn't know what these audio cues and visual signals are, or if you do not use them, then practice together so you will both know. The Queen should ask you if you understand after she's given you cues. Once you confirm your understanding, then you accept that your Queen will use signals to show you how she feels. Naturally, you must always work to please your Queen and make her happy. I hope you see where this is going.

The meaning of 'purely positive' tends to vary according to who is using it. Some *Love & Obey* female trainers use it, as I mentioned, as a way of signaling both positive and negative messages. Others use it only as a positive reinforcement, or at least, as much as possible. And some only use it when they are angry.

The term 'purely positive' implies that trainers use no unpleasant stimuli and don't create "non-events" that lack reinforcement. Both non-events and negative punishment are used by some *Love & Obey* female trainers, and BOTH are negative. A non-event is every bit as negative as punishment, sometimes even more so. All negative reinforcement techniques are not created equal. Some are mild and some are severe.

Some trainers use negative reinforcement and some don't. Some say, "No" or make an "ughhh" sound; some don't. Some use physical punishers like spanking and some don't. Some use negative reinforcement in various ways and some don't. Some use all of the above in real life but without teaching it. Each woman has to decide what she wants to do and how her man responds to it. Some Queens and their men like to be placed over a woman's knees and spanked with her hand or a paddle. Others prefer "time outs" or taking away certain privileges, like watching a favorite TV show. The point is, each woman must communicate the concept to her man in a simple, meaningful way. I am in charge; you must seek approval and avoid at all costs my disapproval. You must always seek approval because the rewards are great. This puts your woman as the authority and keeps life running smoothly. *When mama's happy, everybody's happy!*

When I described the results of this experiment to a woman in a female led relationship in Texas, she laughed and said, "I have worked out the perfect signal to tell my man that he has done the right thing is to simply say, 'Momma's Happy!' And when he misbehaves, I tell him, 'Momma's not happy.' Believe me, he understands what's comin' both ways."

No method of man teaching is purely positive. By scientific definition, the removal of a desired reward is a negative punishment. So, if you ever withhold a reward, such as "no orgasming for you for a month" or use a "time-out," by scientific definition, you are a trainer who uses negative techniques or punishment to train your man. A negative punishment indicates that something has been taken away from the man to achieve a reduction in the bad behavior. However, unlike BDSM/FEMDOM, no harsh whipping or disgusting "shitting in his mouth" techniques are needed or used in a loving Female Led Relationship. You can simply offer a "time out" or no "blow jobs for a month." And that is punishment enough.

You simply do not need to lock a man in a cage or beat him with a whip or humiliate or sissify him. I don't agree with it, like or condone it. I hope the goal for those reading this book is to return to a romantic, honeymoon-like state of relationship bliss and not to be a cruel Queen from the dark side. *Love & Obey* Queens are in large part "kind and loving." If your goal is to practice dark BDSM, move on and stop reading my book. I want people who are looking for a loving and respectful relationship and who understand that women are superior to men, and relationships better off when a woman is in charge.

CHAPTER 11

> "A man must know that he can only be a woman's true love if he is obedient and does what she commands."
>
> — Marisa Rudder

Note: *Don't worry that your woman knows you are reading about techniques she will use to train you. Even though both of you may know what is happening in the obedience training, it doesn't matter because you both want to achieve the same goal—a loving Female Led Relationship, so naturally you are both open and willing to share these ideas. Again, if you have no woman yet, read these alone and share later.*

We love our men and need to train them in a loving way! I, for one, can't imagine life without a man. I admire and love men for all their wonderful qualities like loyalty, affection, playfulness, humor, sexuality and their zest for life. Nevertheless, men are very different from women. Although, officially I can say, "Men, you can't live with us, and you can't live without us!" However, we can live with you once you agree to the Female Led lifestyle. You won't believe the life transformations, and how stress and conflict disappears. If you have some innocent but irksome tendencies—like leaving the toilet seat up, not cleaning up after yourself, making stupid comments, not doing chores, not opening doors, not pulling out chairs and not following commands—that can make it downright difficult for a dominant woman to live with you! To make the most of your relationship with your woman, you need to learn some important skills and become a gentleman who will help you live harmoniously with her lifestyle goals and personal desires.

Learning obedience and how to be a gentleman will improve your life, as well as hers. Being a gentleman will enhance the bond between you, and ensure her well-being. And it will be a lot of fun! If you are reading this book, you are probably eager to learn, and the key to success is described in one word—obedience. Your Queen must communicate how she'd like you to behave and why it's in your best interest to obey her commands and wishes. If she doesn't, ask her politely to try and do this for you.

How Should You Let Your Queen Lead?

Again, please share this section with your wife or girlfriend, *if she is ready to accept her role as your Queen.* A search on the Internet will show all kinds of advice about Female Led Relationships and how to make a man obey and serve you. Some people will tell you that the key is to use a "firm hand" to make sure your man doesn't think he can get away with any bad behavior. They will use the term "dominatrix" to describe a dominant woman, which often confuses people to assume a Female Led Relationship is naturally a BDSM/FEMDOM relationship when it is not the same at all.

I believe that a woman's power comes from love. We are the channels of love from the universe and we should use loving female techniques and rewards in teaching, and avoid punishing our men, except in symbolic, soft ways like a light spanking over the knees, if that is something you enjoy. I also believe that it is important for the woman to change her attitude, and this takes time, but she must become "the loving female authority figure," and assert her status as the dominant leader of your relationship. It's easy to get overwhelmed by the differing opinions on the Internet about the Female Led Relationship but it is simpler than you think.

Simply follow the *Love & Obey* system to achieve a loving female relationship, which is really what most couples are after. One of the most frequent complaints of women in any relationship is that their man "just won't listen." But if she puts herself in her man's shoes for a minute, she might sympathize. For instance, if someone was constantly talking to her about an issue she has no clue about, it would not be long before she loses interest—think about it, how long would anyone pay attention? If she is not a football fan, her man's strategy sport talks would most likely not catch her attention. To put it simply, a person wouldn't be able to understand what is being communicated to them unless they happen to be knowledgeable of the subject, such as football.

To communicate clearly and consistently with your man, women need to understand how he learned to be the way he is in the first place. Men learn through the immediate consequences of their behavior. The nature of those consequences determines how they'll behave in the future. Men, like women, work to achieve positive aspects and avoid bad outcomes in life. If a man's behavior results in a reward like money, sex, a fun night out on the town, or winning at your favorite sport, then he will proceed with that behavior more often. On the other hand, if a behavior results in an unpleasant consequence, like being ignored by his friends, not getting laid, losing money or going to jail, then he will reduce behaving in that manner.

Some Female Led Relationship teaching methods use BDSM/FEMDOM methods to achieve an exchange of power in the relationship. I have mentioned before that this is simply not my thing, and I don't like it or think it is truly conducive to a loving relationship. Punishment is an element that some couples incorporate into their Female Led Relationships. Punishment is used to correct unwanted behavior, and some dominant women strive to find the perfect punishment. The following stricter style of punishments are ideas for you to see if some of these techniques will work for your relationship. Physical punishment includes any spanking, paddling, caning or another impactful tool. If you don't have a tool, you can use your hand to spank or slap your man. An effective way to discipline includes having your man count out the spankings, which becomes difficult as you increase the intensity. Hand spanking can be adjusted so it won't really hurt him, but it will send a message.

If the Queen likes being strict and believes that punishment is effective for teaching her man, then here are some forms of punishment I have implemented on occasion that are not hardcore, nasty or dangerous in nature but work very effectively.

1. Try mental bondage, which requires the man to stay in the same place for a specified amount of time, and is similar to a "time-out." Breaking from the position could warrant another punishment (as long as it's something he should be able to do).

2. Kneeling is a form of punishment that is particularly popular. Instruct him to kneel at your feet or in the corner; it will be uncomfortable but does no lasting damage, so it makes a good form of discipline when he has broken the rules. Kneeling before you also establish your authority over him. At the end, you can ask him if he is ready to be released and ready to kiss your feet and apologize for his bad behavior.

3. Another good but non-violent technique is restrictive discipline, which simply means you take something away that he likes. It could be as simple as grounding or removing mobile phone or TV privileges, or even forbidding him to eat his favorite food. In addition, when he is not allowed to watch TV, the woman should watch

his least favorite shows like *Girlfriends' Guide to Divorce* or *Fleabag*.

4. Not being able to sleep in the same room as you, making him sit on the floor and not use furniture, not allowing him to make eye contact, or making him crawl all evening and not walk upright are other restrictions to consider. Once your man has shown he is properly remorseful, he can retreat to his privileges.

5. Consider two old school teacher's or nun's methods, if you attended catholic school like me. A lecture might accompany these punishments, and it might be the only discipline that's needed. Plus, there may be no more fitting punishment than requiring your man to write, "I will not do the "forbidden action" 100 times on a piece of paper.

6. Another favorite punishment is to make your man do something he does opposes doing. What chore does your man hate doing? Perhaps washing the dishes or scrubbing the toilet? What better way to punish him, then to do those chores! Errand running is another option.

As I mentioned, I prefer to focus on the positive most of the time and cut right to the chase, and focus on teaching my man what I want him to do. While both tactics can work, the latter is usually the more loving and effective approach, and it's also much more enjoyable for the couple. For example, the woman can easily use rewards and verbal praise or reinforcement combined with sexual rewards to teach a man that certain actions are positive and will be rewarded. This is a positive way to teach him to love, obey and serve you.

Teaching games that can be played with a man to perform general skills, such as teaching/training him how to give a kick-ass massage, perform world-class cunnilingus, or running your bath the way you like it. It can be any particular skill, like cooking or cleaning, or manicuring and pedicuring. If the woman isn't available to teach, then there are schools he can attend to learn. There are schools to teach just about all of the techniques that I am going to discuss.

Most men are "doers" and like to be active, and the secret is to use the desire to her benefit. For females, the secret is to get your man to be in active service to you, such as cooking, cleaning the house, performing oral sex, or giving a manicure or massage.

It is crucial to give praise to the man when he performs these tasks. "Honey, that was the best oral you have ever done, and you're becoming an amazing lover!" Or say, "That was such a delicious chicken parmigiana dinner. You're such a great chef!" If you are particularly impressed with his effort, give him the big reward. After the verbal praise, it is a good idea to let him have sex with you. Your verbal praise reinforces good behavior and is called "conditioning," which is a behavioral process; whereby a response becomes more frequent or more predictable in a given environment as a result of reinforcement. With reinforcement being a typical stimulus or reward for a desired action.

Why is sex or the blow job such a great reward? Most women know that the big reward all men love and makes them sexually addicted is a phenomenal blow job, giving him a full-body, shaking orgasm. If the female doesn't know how to do it already, then I suggest learning some techniques (plenty of videos online) to keep the man addicted and deeply devoted, as well as having a lot of fun in the bedroom. Announcing his big reward will define fellatio as a big reward, which he earned for being extra good.

In an FLR, a man's rewards are the only time a Queen will focus on his sexual pleasure. Plus, when she allows him to get pleasure in this way, his "measure of himself as a man" heightens. He is pleasured in the most intimate place. A deep and vulnerable desire is met. When choosing to learn exactly what he craves and pleasure enthusiastically, he feels manly, sexy and powerful. A man's need for sex is not wrong. On the contrary, it is part of a woman's plan. The sexual experience fills his heart no other area can fulfill. Nature designed sex to draw a couple together in unity like nothing else can. With a healthy diet of generous sex in a marriage, he feels emotionally satisfied. However, I must mention that over time, selfish sex and the blow job is often replaced by a desire to serve the female. So, don't be surprised if he asks, "Can I go down on you instead of getting a blow job?" It happens and then you know your man is very well trained.

Eventually, your well-trained man's reward will become letting him go down on you, and these rewards will have many benefits outside the bedroom. There's something incredibly intimate about getting oral, which is probably what makes the ac feel so good. If your man is familiar with your private parts and regularly spends time with them, chances are he is extremely comfortable with you outside the bedroom as well. Oral sex creates sexual intimacy, which leads to emotional intimacy (and vice versa). Once your man learns to love giving you oral even more than receiving it, he will feel closer and be more vulnerable with his emotions. This will create better communication and increased emotional intimacy for you both.

I also encourage giving him rewards like a seductive dance or a strip show, or wearing sexy lingerie to start things off. Your curves excite him in ways unimaginable. Even if you feel downright ridiculous, he appreciates your body and your ways of enticing him. Everyone has insecurities about their bodies, but don't let that hold you back from giving him the ecstasy he so desires. You're sexier than you think! As a *Love & Obey* Queen, you will see what happens when he gets a reward, especially the blow job or strip tease dance. When you reward your man in this way more regularly, the trash gets taken out, the dishes get done, and you will do much less housework. This psycho-sexual hold over men is the secret of the Female Led Relationship. Once a man's orgasms and penis are controlled, he will attempt anything for his reward. You'll be surprised to see how your man suddenly feels motivated to do things for you when you are only giving him sexual favors when he behaves obediently. A good sex life is a powerful force in a Female Led Relationship.

Classical conditioning is best understood using the example of Pavlov's dog. The scientist rang a bell each time he fed the dog. After a while, the sound of the bell became entangled with the concept of food in the dog's brain and upon hearing the bell, it would begin to salivate. This is known as a conditioned response.

The really simple translation to your man's teaching is that if a particular audio signal like "snapping your fingers" or even a verbal expression, like "I want a massage," or "make me dinner tonight," and the man knows he is accomplishing your desires, he will be rewarded with sexual pleasure. Then the sounds of those fingers snapping or your verbal commands will eventually start to elicit an arousing response, even if it is not a sexual activity that you request. My man becomes aroused when I tell him to prepare the throne, which means laying out pillows and blankets I've shown him how to do; thus, he associates it with me relaxing, reading or watching TV, and then ultimately in him being allowed to perform oral sex and possibly even intercourse. Verbal praise and sex are simply the two fool-proof ways to train a man and having him become your obedient gentleman for life.

Again, make sure you share this with your woman, even though both of you may know what is happening in the obedience training. It doesn't matter because you both want to achieve the same goal—a loving Female Led Relationship, so naturally you are both open to these ideas.

Remember, all *Love & Obey* teaching boils down to this simple system of rewards and punishments. Or, more accurately, it is everything that the Queen does, which either encourages or discourages certain behaviors, whether intentional or not. This can come from your body language, facial expressions, words you use when you talk to them, if you use their real name when angry or pet name when pleased, maintaining eye contact when speaking, and pretty much every other thing you ever do, every day. Experiencing some sort of pressure will be worth earning great rewards. This conditioning is the use of consequences to modify the voluntary behavior of the man by associating choices and behavior that end in a defined set of consequences.

As mentioned in the beginning, we all condition each other constantly; it is not wrong or manipulative. It is simply the way people interact with each other. When you see another man do something and say, "Oh boy, his wife is going to kill me." That is the result of a pattern of actions that have established an expectation in you about the results of your future actions. On a positive social level, men are "hopefully" trained to have manners, like when a man holds a door for a woman and she says thank you without thinking about it—that's conditioning. It is subtle, subconscious, and totally unnoticed, even by the person doing it. But it is real and it is happening every second of every day. What you need to do is train away bad male led behavior with negative consequences (no sex), and reward good female led behavior with sexual rewards. Remember my simple line, "If you love me, you will obey me!"

If you can teach your man polite manners without hurting or frightening him, why not do it? Rather than punishing him for all the things you don't want him to do, concentrate on teaching your man what he should be doing. When your man does something favorable, convince him to do it again by rewarding him with something he loves. You'll get the job done without damaging the relationship between you and your man. And it doesn't take long, our brains are programmed to pick up on these patterns very quickly and adapt to them. In fact, before the end of the first week, a woman can usually teach a man to comply with her commands and perform several positive behaviors.

The human brain constantly collects information from others around us to determine what is expected of us and what we can expect from others. How many of you have been to a large convention? You go to get your badge, and you all go to the desk that has the first letter of your name on it. If there is a line, you wait patiently until it's your turn. No one has to tell you to do that. You just know that it is expected of you. And if you want to effectively teach your man obedience, then be mindful of consistent actions that lets him know what is expected of him and what his expectations are from his woman. And you never have to say a single thing out loud about it, if you don't want to. Effective teaching can be done with simple rewards for good behavior, and negative consequences for bad behavior.

If You Don't Like the Behavior, Take Rewards Away.

The most important part of teaching your man is teaching him that it pays to do things you like. But your man also needs to learn that it doesn't pay to do things you don't like. Fortunately, discouraging unwanted behavior doesn't have to involve pain or intimidation. You just need to make sure that behavior you dislike doesn't get rewarded. Most of the time, male motivations aren't mysterious. They simply do what works! Men tell us we look beautiful, for example, because we return compliments with positive attention (perhaps a kiss). They can learn not to give compliments if we ignore them when they compliment us. It can be as simple as turning away or staring at the sky when your man praises you. Or you can reward him with if he flatters you with the attention he craves, like a loving kiss.

If you stick to this plan, your man will learn two things at once. Doing something you like (complimenting, etc.) reliably works to earn what he wants (attention), and doing things you don't like (being rude) always results in the loss of what he wants. When your man is rude, raises his voice or acts in a displeasing way, give him the cold shoulder, and tell him to go to his room and think about his behavior. Or in a more well-trained man, instruct him to get down on his knees at your feet. Make him wait until you forgive him and then allow him to kiss your feet before he is allowed to stand up again.

Consequences Must Be Immediate.

Men live in the present. Unlike us, they don't necessarily think about connections between events and experiences that are separated by long periods of time. For your man to connect something he does with the consequences of his behavior, the consequences must be immediate. If you want to discourage your man from doing something, you have to catch him with his hand in the "cookie jar." For example, if your man does not perform his household chores, but asks you to have sex, tell him immediately, "You did not do your chores, so no sex for you." The message is immediate and clear: No chores completed, no sex for you. You'll notice he won't miss doing his chores after that. Likewise, rewards for good behavior must come right after that behavior has happened, as well. So be prepared to reward your man with praise, petting and sex the instant he does something right—like his chores.

Consequences must be consistent. When teaching your man, you should respond the same way to things he does every time he does them. For example, if you sometimes kiss and get into petting your man when he gets up from the couch to greet you but sometimes you yell at him to leave you alone, he's going to become confused. How can he know when it's okay to greet you and when it's not?

Be a Good Leader.

Some people believe that the only way to transform a disobedient man into a well-behaved one is to dominate him and show him who's boss. However, the "alpha female" concept in man teaching is risky at times. More importantly, it leads females to use corporal punishment techniques that aren't always safe, like the "beatings." Men who are forcibly beaten and held down can become frightened and confused, and they're sometimes driven to fight back in self-defense.

Keep in mind that the "loving female authority" concept doesn't mean you have to let your man do anything he likes. It's important to be the boss and make the rules, but you can do that without unnecessary physical punishment. Be a kind and loving girl boss; not a bully. Good leadership isn't about cruel dominance, but it can also be kind dominance. It's about controlling your man's behavior by controlling his access to things he wants. YOU have what he wants. Let's face it ladies, he wants pussy, and as long as you're the one with the pussy, you can make the rules. You must know your power and how to use it. Make him know that good behavior results in getting pussy and bad behavior results in not getting any. Use your lady part to your best advantage.

If your man wants to do something, make him do something you want before you allow it. When he wants dinner, and you make dinner, ask him to massage your feet for a few minutes to earn it. Does he want to go see a movie? Does he want to go to a sporting event? Does he want to get some new tools, or electronic device? Does he eagerly want to have sex with you? Your man will happily work for everything he loves in life, if he is trained properly. Your man must simply be taught to do what you want in order to get what he wants. Listen ladies, you know what he wants, whether it's watching football, getting laid, or being fed. So, every time he asks for it, make sure he does something you want first, until he gets it. Soon, he will know that he needs to do what you want to get what he wants. It is pretty simple really.

Teaching New Skills.

It's easy to reward good behavior if you focus on teaching your man to do specific things you like. Men can learn an endless array of obedience skills and entertaining activities that bring female's great pleasure. Deciding what you'd like your man to learn will depend on your interests and lifestyle. If you want your man to behave politely, you can focus on manners and etiquette, such as opening doors, pulling out chairs, and to come to your service when called. If you want to enhance your enjoyment of city activities with your man, you can focus on your shopping and lunch outings. If you have a high-energy man and you also like outdoor activities, you can teach him to get everything ready for surfing, camping, sporting, skiing, tennis, golf, or other sporty activities of your choice. If you'd like to impress your girlfriends with your training skills and just spend some quality time with your man, you can take him to female activities like getting a mani-pedi or going to the spa with you and the girls. The possibilities are endless! Just remember to reward him for good behavior.

One more note, be sure to reward your man with whatever he truly finds rewarding. As I mentioned, sex is fool-proof, but sporting event tickets, playing video games, electronic device gifts, tools or sports equipment are also excellent rewards. Withholding his permission to orgasm for a while, if he hasn't ejaculated in a while, he'll probably enthusiastically do anything you ask to be allowed his sexual release. Be patient, teaching your man will take time and effort, but it can be a great deal of fun for you. And your hard work will pay off. With patience and persistence, you and your man can accomplish a beautiful Female Led Relationship.

CHAPTER 12

> "A man must learn that love means doing what your woman has commanded you, and she has commanded you to love and obey her, and to be good and to serve her."
>
> – Marisa Rudder

In this chapter, I will discuss warning signs and traits that a woman will look out for and how to change them in yourself. Remember, that all men are **not** created equal and some will be decidedly less appealing to women than others. Remember the golden rule, if you love a woman, you will obey her. Obedience is a higher form of love. However, if you exhibit the following signs, you are telling a woman that you may be difficult to train and will not be good in a Female Led Relationship. Women look for these warning signs and if you're up to it, try and get rid of these traits before you search for a dominant woman. If you don't make any progress quickly, you may be better off to wait before trying to get a woman to join you in a Female Led Relationship. Here are some definite warning signs you need to look for in yourself.

1. If you fail to ask questions about your woman and her feelings or pretend like you care about her feelings. Ideally, women like a man who cares about who they are as a person and why they want certain things in life. You need to work on sympathy and empathy.

2. If a woman is in the middle of a conversation and you always look at your phone, another woman or the scenery, and pretend like you have seen something so urgent that you must respond to it while she is speaking. You need to work on your listening skills.

3. If you never laugh at her jokes and stories. I don't expect every man on earth to think women are comedians, but people who don't laugh at all are frustrating. Plus, if you never laugh at anything your woman says, she will probably feel like you hate her sense of humor or you have no humor, and either way, that's a turn-off. So, work on finding the "ha-ha" in her jokes.

4. If you look anywhere but in her direction when she is talking to you. If you are just unable to look at her for more than thirty seconds at a time, it is unacceptable. If you're talking, you have to be willing to look at her and listen. If not, it just won't work. Communication is really important to women.

5. If you can't stop talking about one thing that honestly doesn't matter, you have a problem. It's great that you love your job or CrossFit or Xbox, but if you have zero interest outside of one particular area, it will be maddening to a woman. Because if she doesn't love Xbox too, and the only source of conversation you have are video games, your relationship is going nowhere.

6. If you smell like you gave up on the concept of showering, you have an issue. *Love and Obey* women like metrosexual men who care about their appearance and personal hygiene. I know everyone's body smells from

time to time and no one's perfect, but women will not keep going out you if you smell bad. If you're too lazy to shower, and put on cologne to disguise your stench, she might want to hold her nose around you because you smell like a dumpster alley cat. All I'm saying is, take five minutes to wash, brush your teeth comb your hair, put on a clean shirt, socks and underwear. Gentleman need to be well-groomed and hygienic. That's what women like. You need to look nice, smell nice and act nice to get started.

7. If you say stupid misogynistic comments like, "You're not like the other girls because you're funny, cool and smart." Wow, those kind of misogynist comments are a big turnoff to FLR women who are usually feminists. What are you really saying when you make a comment like that? Most women aren't funny or cool or smart or whatever other thing you're trying to compliment her on? Because guess what? All of this woman's friends pretty much have all the qualities that she has, and she is thinking you sound like an idiot right now.

8. If she asks you to hang out with your friends, but then you make no effort to include her, so she is just stuck wondering if this guy even likes you. And if you don't break the ice and help her to connect with your friends, then they end up having no idea why she is even there. Remember ultimately, you are heading for a relationship where she is the most important person in the world to you. So, you need to put her as the number one priority from the beginning.

9. If he calls his ex "crazy" you are again falling into dark misogynistic territory. Women believe that when you call your ex "crazy," it actually is just code for calling all women insane for not doing what you want. This is far from living to worship women. This also means that she will believe one day you'll call her crazy. So, most women

will not mess with men who say misogynistic comments about other women. Stop doing it immediately.

10. Once again, if she doesn't think you care about the way you look. No one's perfect, but I know so many guys who wear stained T-shirts they got as a gift when they were thirteen years old, and say some junk like Dallas Fun Run 2008. These men clearly don't care, which usually also translates to their poor-fitting jeans and stupid dad sneakers with barely tied laces. Female led women like well-dressed men who care about looking good for them. You don't have to love fashion and it's okay to just be yourself, but guys who couldn't care less about being well-dressed and looking presentable on a date (especially when women are expected to do a ton of date prep) is a really difficult man to train for a Female Led Relationship. FLR women are stylish and educated for the most, part and they want the same in their men.

11. If you have long, dirty finger or toe nails. Not only is it gross but also your chances of getting anywhere near a *Love & Obey* woman's body with your filthy animal claws just went from slim to none. So, learn how to groom yourself or get a professional stylist to give you a makeover before you start dating. Or just look online at metrosexual men and start studying how they groom, dress and present themselves.

12. If you list all the books, movies and music you like and there's not a single female lead actress, female singer like Rhianna, or book with a romantic theme, or you even say something stupid like, "I don't like girly stuff," it makes you a terrible candidate for a dominant female lifestyle in her mind. If on the other hand you say, "Art made by women is the best." It will show her that you have a brain and good taste.

With great power comes the responsibility to think, act and look like a Queen. So, if you are looking for a Goddess or a Queen, consider the following:

1. Make sure you look for a *Love & Obey* Queen who stands out from the crowd. Look for a woman who has good manners. A dominant woman is not a mean or rude person. Instead, she makes an effort to empower all women. She ignores women who are nasty and rude, and goes about her life on her own terms, maintaining her sense of elegance and projecting class.

2. A *Love & Obey* Queen dresses with good taste, and although she can be sexy, she does it with dignity and not in a trashy way. She does not have to wear only designer clothes, but her clothes will be in style, complimentary in color, clean, pressed and will actually fit her right.

3. A *Love & Obey* Queen is meticulously clean and well-groomed every day. Her hair is styled and her nails are manicured and pedicured. She cares for her skin and she has no body odor.

4. A *Love & Obey* Queen not only says, "Hello" she adds, "It's a pleasure to meet you." She says, "No, thank you," or "Yes, please." She does not respond with a "yea, yup, nope or nah." She calls her elders "sir" or "ma'am." When she addresses a man, it is always as "Mr. (last name)" and a woman as "Mrs." or "Miss (last name)" until they've been green-lighted to use their first name or nickname. Look for a woman with manners and you will see a powerful woman.

5. A *Love & Obey* Queen is prepared to lead a lifestyle, reads and keeps up with the world news, and makes an effort to speak intelligently. Look for women who speak intelligently about world events.

6. When a *Love & Obey* Queen receives an invitation, she promptly RSVPs or declines. When she receives help or hospitality from someone, she thanks them to display her gratitude. When she attends a gathering, she does not arrive empty-handed or late. She brings a small hostess gift. So, when you see women like this, you have found a *Love & Obey* Queen.

7. A *Love & Obey* Queen knows her worth and knows she deserves to be pursued. She does not call a man. If you feel the need to have a woman initiate contact, she will know that she is not dealing with a gentleman and should move on. Look for a woman who has a high opinion of herself.

8. A *Love & Obey* Queen is actively listening and engaging in conversations and speaks with confidence and clearly enough for others to understand her. She is polite and well-mannered and demands the same from her men, but she only gives compliments when she sincerely means it.

9. A *Love & Obey* Queen seeks the truth and questions everything she hears. She defends the truth even when it's unpopular. She has strong opinions, a sense of right and wrong, and is passionate about her point-of-view.

10. A *Love & Obey* Queen is dignified. She may get upset and angry, everyone does, but she knows how to stay calm. She responds to the issue and does not make personal attacks.

So, remember, you are looking for a unique woman when you are looking for a Queen. She is usually a high-maintenance woman, and to maintain your appeal and attraction to her, you must impress her. Think of a Queen and begin to carry yourself in a manner that would attract a woman like that. Read books and watch movies about powerful women, and study their style and manners. These are women who have a power over men and know how to control men. She is a woman who will quickly demand obedience, so you must show her that you are ready to be a gentleman and deliver excellence. The rewards of this lifestyle are great but there are demands as well.

CHAPTER 13

> "A man must obey his Queen, and do what she says. A woman's work is to watch over her man, and as woman, you are accountable for his care. A man must give his woman a reason to love him with joy and not with pain. That would certainly not be in a man's best interest."
>
> – Marisa Rudder

Now back to teaching you how to behave properly. When you were a child, you were most likely happy when your parents gave you a dollar for every "A" on your report card. They made you want to get all "A's," right? That's a good example of positive reinforcement. Men care about praise, success, sex...and food. Use positive reinforcement and teach your man with praise and rewards when he does something you want him to do. Because the reward makes him more likely to repeat the behavior, positive reinforcement is one of your most powerful tools for shaping or changing your man's behavior. Rewarding your man for good behavior sounds pretty simple, and it is! But to practice the technique effectively, you need to follow some basic guidelines.

Timing is everything in life and training.

Correct timing is essential when using positive reinforcement.

- The reward must occur immediately—within seconds—or your man may not associate it with the proper action. For example, if you have your man cook dinner but reward him after he's finished and watching TV, he'll think he's being rewarded for watching TV.

- Use an audio and visual cue to mark the correct behavior and improve your timing, and also help your man understand the connection between the correct behavior and the reward. Give him an "Attaboy" while he's cooking, plus a loving smile and a kiss.

Keep it short and sweet.

Men need simple polite commands. "Bill, I want you to be a good boy and cook dinner for us now." Keep your commands short and to the point; be polite and keep them uncomplicated.

Consistency is key.

You should use the same commands; otherwise, your man may be confused. It might help to post a list of commands where you both can see them. Consistency also means only rewarding the desired behavior and never rewarding any undesired behavior.

When to use positive reinforcement.

Positive reinforcement is great for teaching your man about your commands, and it's also a good way of reinforcing his good behavior.

Give him a smile, kiss or a "Good boy" for taking a shower, straightening up around the house or bringing you a cup of coffee in the morning. But be careful that you don't mistakenly use positive reinforcement to reward unwanted behaviors. For example, if you let your man make love to you every time he begs you for some, or when he acts grumpy because you haven't given him any in a day or two, you're giving him a reward for behavior you want to discourage. You need to be in control. Don't let begging or acting grumpy get a reward. You can call him on it and explain that he'll be allowed to make love to you when you want him to, and he will be cheerful and will not beg you for it or it will only prolong his time without a reward. Tell him you don't like begging or grumpy moods around the house. Then when he acts cheerful and surprises you with something thoughtful, reward him.

Shaping behavior can take time.

You may need to use a technique called "shaping," which means reinforcing something close to the desired response and then gradually requiring more from your man before he gets a big reward. For example, if you're teaching your man cleanliness, you may initially reward him for just showering or just shaving. Then you may want him to add deodorant, cologne, hair gel, and finally for being totally well-groomed and looking sharp.

Types of rewards.

Positive reinforcement can include verbal praise, light petting, kissing or a warm smile, sexual rewards and food rewards. Since most men are highly food-motivated, telling him that your fixing his favorite meatloaf or lasagna or steak for dinner can work especially well for rewarding him for good behavior.

- Food rewards should be enticing and irresistible to your man. Experiment a bit to see which rewards work best.

- Another reward can be taking him to his favorite place, like the sports bar to watch the game. You can even combine the rewards like telling him, "Let's go to your favorite sports bar and watch the game their tonight and get a pizza or burgers." That can be a great reward, if that's what he likes. You know him best so it should be easy to figure it out. Maybe he likes arcades or miniature golf.

- Each time you use any reward, you should couple it with a verbal reward (praise). Say something like, "Yes, you were a really good boy today, and I really appreciated how you did (something you liked) and I want to give you a special reward for it. Say this in a loving, positive and happy tone of voice. Then give your man his reward.

If your man isn't as motivated by food rewards, sex is guaranteed to be an effective reward. So, you can always give him the same praise and let him know he's going to get lucky tonight!

When to give rewards.

When your man is learning a new behavior, reward him every time he does the new behavior. This is called continuous reinforcement. Once your man has reliably learned the new behavior, you want to switch to intermittent reinforcement, in which you continue with praise, but gradually reduce the number of times he receives a reward for doing the desired behavior.

- In the beginning, reward him with the reward four out of every five times he does the behavior. Over time, reward him three out of five times, then two out of five times, and so on, until you're only rewarding him occasionally.

- Continue to verbally praise him every time—although once your man has learned the behavior, your praise can be sprinkled on when it feels right, such as a quiet but positive, "Attaboy."

- You have to keep praising and rewarding your man. However, you can use a variable schedule of reinforcement so that he doesn't catch on that he only has to respond every other time. Once trained, your man will soon learn that if he keeps responding with good behavior, eventually he'll get what he wants—your praise and a reward. Warning! Don't decrease the rewards too quickly. Especially in the first few months of training. Put yourself out to reward him—you want him thinking that this new Female Led Relationship is fantastic. He should think he's getting laid more than he did in college in the first six months of training.

By understanding positive reinforcement, you'll see that you're not forever bound to have sex on a daily basis, although, many women report the sex becomes so good, they want it more than their men do. In no time at all, your man will soon be looking to you for your verbal praise, because he wants to please you and knows that, occasionally, he'll get a Big Reward, too!

These simple reinforcement methods work and there is scientific data supporting it. For those of you who are not all that familiar with audio and visual teaching, it really is quite simple. It depends upon a little sound or gesture that reinforces good behavior. The man learns that whenever he hears a positive sound "Attaboy" and sees a smile from you, he knows a reward is coming soon after. Or if you "snap your fingers" and give him "the look" that something is going to be taken away from him.

So, the man sets about trying to produce behaviors that cause his woman to give him a "Attaboy" and a smile, knowing that it will be followed by a reward. In so doing the man learns which behavior is wanted by you. Thus, the teaching sequence is quite simple: get him to do the desired behavior; mark that behavior (with a sound and/or gesture); reward the behavior later with food, a gift or a sexual reward.

Your voice and facial expressions will work fine with your man. Choose the ones that best suit your style as a *Love & Obey* Queen. The more that the behavior is repeated and rewarded, the stronger that behavior becomes. In recent years, there has been a lot of attention given to audio and visual teaching which is viewed by some people as a more efficient way of teaching your man. Unfortunately, there is a lot of misunderstanding associated with this method of teaching men. Before I try to clear up some of the confusion associated with audio and visual teaching, it is important to understand that the basic principle behind teaching men is really quite simple. That does not mean that the successful application of this principle will be easy. Remember that the basic principle behind playing the piano is simple, all you have to do is to press the keys corresponding to the notes that you want to hear. However, it takes lots of practice before you can do it right. So, don't get frustrated and stick with it and you will succeed.

The basic principle behind teaching your man any new task is that any behavior awarded will be strengthened and the likelihood that it will appear will increase. While any behavior not rewarded will be weakened and the likelihood that it will appear will decrease. That's it! To train a man, it is not necessary to understand the underlying neurological or chemical events, or know which brain centers and pathways are involved. The "tricky" part; however, is often being able to get the man to perform the behavior in the first place so that we can reward it. It is also necessary to get that reward to him at the right time, so that the appropriate behaviors will be strengthened. This process sometimes requires a fair bit of time and effort. You also need to express what you want to a man in a clear and understandable way.

Most of us have been in a sexual situation where you wanted a man to stop. The ability to say 'stop' when you feel uncomfortable starts with an acknowledgement that you don't owe him anything. In a Female Led Relationship, you get to decide what you do and don't want to do on the physical side of a relationship.

A Female Led Relationship is a full commitment. If he only gives you a half-commitment or he just wants to be friends-with-benefits and that isn't what you want, then ask him to commit. You are your own worst enemy by allowing him to string you along without making a commitment to trying "your kind of relationship" if you don't want to say female led.

You are a *Love & Obey* Queen now and he has to earn the right to touch you or have sex with you, and you are never obligated to do it when you don't want to. Tell him you are going home and don't listen if he begs or gets pissed off, and threatens you that you better stay. Know how to spot compromising situations and get out. That's what taking charge is all about.

Share your desire for him to follow your lead. Don't wait until you have completely lost it to express how you feel. If your man does something that bothers you, tell him. Take the lead and don't be afraid to have little confrontations along the way. A healthy Female Led Relationship is based on good communication. We all disappoint each other, but we must learn to express our feelings before we reach a boiling point.

We all have a past and it's important to be vulnerable with your man and tell him how you feel about the pain you have experienced in your life. Let him in slowly and trust him with your emotions, and reveal anything that is displeasing and unpleasant to you. Also share what makes you happy. See if he takes the cue and gives you what you want. Then reward him for it.

Just say "No." Say he wants you to go home with him, and he grabs your butt and makes an inappropriate joke. As women, we must learn to say "no" and stand up for ourselves. Don't apologize and don't be silent. Let him know that you'll tell him if and when you want him to go home with you and then leave.

Say (when you're sober), "I want to be with you," when you really want it. He isn't a mind reader. Use your words and express your desires. You'll want to say it to the right man one day. You can't expect him to read your mind, so step up to the plate and tell him how you feel. Chances are that the man you love will struggle with his own identity. Maybe he had a career failure or maybe it's because of some criticism he's been hearing. Look him in his eyes and tell him he has what it takes. Tell him that you believe in him.

My (career, faith, children, etc.) is really important to me. Don't change your desires into those of your man of the moment. Stand up for who you are and what you believe in. Don't apologize for being you. A relationship is never worth compromising the core of who you are. Be a *Love & Obey* Queen and set the standards in your relationship.

In our digital world, feel free to text, "Please stop contacting me." Or "No I won't send you a pic." Or "No I won't come over at 11pm." You shouldn't have to live in fear of the next angry text you'll receive. Tell him upfront not to contact you anymore because you need to give yourself time to breathe and get over it. If he threatens to break up with you because you won't send him a picture, then delete him from your phone and move on. The right man won't make demands from you of which you aren't comfortable with. You can warn him first, but if he still sends the 10 p.m. "where are you?" booty call text—- let him know that doesn't cut it for you. Meeting up with him at the last minute will only reinforce his bad behavior and the anxiety pumping through your body awaiting his text is toxic. Tell him to make a plan and that the last-minute text just won't work for you. In a world where arguments, breakups, and threats are common over text message and social media, know how to cut off an on-screen conversation and demand face-to-face. If he is a real man, he won't hide behind a screen and he'll talk to you in person.

Let him know right away if his behavior is acceptable unacceptable. You have to set standards from the start. Men respect women with standards. So, don't be afraid to set your standards as high as you want. Set standards for your romantic life and know how to express them in a kind, yet strong and straightforward way.

Your love doesn't define me, my love will define you. You are not defined by a man; women ultimately define their man in a Female Led Relationship. Define yourself as a special woman and don't let his changing desires steal your confidence, self-esteem or happiness.

When it comes to learning, young females learn to survive and what is safe, and what they are expected to do - usually from their mothers. If they had to learn only by trial and error and by interacting with the world and making mistakes, many would suffer injuries, and many more would simply die. For this reason, females who live in social groupings benefit from "social learning."

Simply put, social learning refers to the fact that young individuals watch the behavior of more experienced individuals, usually their mother, and from them, they learn which behaviors are most likely to bring them rewards and which behaviors to avoid. It is a reasonable assumption that evolution predisposed young children to observe the behaviors of their elders of their own species in order to safely learn new behaviors. Thus, we know that young children observe human family members in order to learn more about their environments. However, things are complex for domesticated men. They have usually evolved in an urban human environment, and it is extremely complex, with lots of important information that must be learned.

With high divorce rates in most western societies, females are generally taking the leadership role in raising the children. Even in families with two parents, the female is generally the leader in training the children in our modern world. Both man and female individuals can provide essential information which is valuable for the child's safety and happiness but usually the mother is leading the way. Given the complex social world that people grow up in, you have to ask yourself the question, "Do most young children that you know learn from observing the behaviors of their mother or their fathers?" In my experience, the mothers are the leaders in education and guiding the children. Father's generally seem to add to the mix their unique flavor which is good, but the ultimate responsibility seems to fall on the shoulders of the mother.

If children were simply allowed to explore the world and to manipulate it in a trial-and-error fashion, I believe only about 50 percent of them would actually manage to survive to adulthood. However, when they are allowed to see their mother solving day-to-day tasks and getting the daily routine accomplished, they have an opportunity to learn what to do without actually having to fool around with the trial-and-error method themselves. Typically, the demonstrator of most daily activities to the child in the modern urban society is the mother. The modern demonstrator mother has been trained for years and often by her mother on how to efficiently survive in the modern world. The children then get a chance to observe their demonstrator take on different trials and succeed. At the end of this observation period, the children try and go into similar trials and achieve success for themselves, following the teaching of the mothers.

Having the chance to observe the demonstrator mother solving the problem definitely provides a benefit for the observing children. There is a general likelihood that children learn to solve most modern-day social problems from observing their mothers in various social trials and situations. The children see what works for the mother and this leads to an improvement in the success rate for them. It turns out that this result is probably due to the fact that most modern children are more likely to spend more time with their mother than the typical father.

It is important to note that children are not simply imitating the behavior of the adult female authority of the mother, but rather extracting important life information about how the world works, including the fact that women are usually their teachers and leaders from the beginning of their lives.

Even most of the research on parenting in the United States has surveyed mothers, but not fathers. Although, there has been a recent surge of interest in the father's role because more men are now staying at home and raising children today than in the past as women enter the workforce. There are also discrepancies between men's and women's reports about their relative involvement in raising their children. A 1999 University of Maryland study explored these discrepancies by asking a sample of mothers and fathers about five domains of parenting: discipline, play, emotional support, monitoring of activities and playmates, and basic care. Parents were asked: "Ideally, who should discipline children, mainly the mother, mainly the father, or both equally?" Similarly, respondents were also asked: "In parenting your children, who disciplines the children, mainly you, mainly the child's father/mother, or both parents equally?" Questions were repeated for each domain of childrearing and were asked for both parents who currently had children in the home, as well as parents who had adult children.

There is overwhelming consensus between men and women that parenting should be shared equally across most domains. For four of the areas— disciplining children, playing with children, providing emotional support, and monitoring activities and friends—at least 90 percent of men and women say these parenting domains should be shared equally. More than two-thirds of men and women say that caring for children's needs should be shared equally by mothers and fathers.

However, and this is key, when parents' reports the actual involvement, the statistics do not agree. Mothers are far more likely than fathers to be the main disciplinarian of children (47 percent, compared with 17 percent), and that it is mainly the mother who plays with children (37 percent, compared with 14 percent). Similarly, mothers are far more likely than fathers to report that the mother provides most of the emotional support of children (45 percent, compared with 24 percent) and that the mother is the one who mainly monitors their children's activities (51 percent, compared with 27 percent). More mothers than fathers believe that mothers are the main caretakers of children (70 percent vs. 58 percent). Overall, fathers want to believe, and are far more likely to hold the view that domains are shared equally with their partners, while mothers are much more likely to report and statistically shown to be the parent that is primarily involved in rearing their children.

Remember, this last statistical picture was based on male/female households. Single motherhood is now becoming the new "norm" and is no longer once limited to poor women and minorities. This prevalence is due in part to the growing trend of children born outside marriage—a societal trend that was virtually unheard-of decades ago. About four out of ten children are now born to unwed mothers. Nearly two-thirds are born to mothers under the age of thirty. Today, one in four children under the age of eighteen—a total of about 17.2 million—are being raised without a father. Of all single-parent families in the U.S., single mothers make up the majority. According to 2017 U.S. Census Bureau, four out of about twelve million single parent families with children under the age of eighteen, more than 80 percent were headed by single mothers. Around half of single mothers have never married, 29 percent are divorced, 21 percent are either separated or widowed. Half have one child; 30

percent have two. About two-thirds are White, one-third Black, one-quarter Hispanic.

This demonstrates that most young children learn more from observing a mother's behavior in the home environment, even though a father can potentially have influence; it is becoming less common. I believe that this is leading to the shift in the dynamic that women should lead in relationships and in the home environment, as well as the world. It would be sensible for evolution to have programmed young children to watch the actions of their parents to improve the likelihood of their survival. But now, the crucial question remains: Since females have evolved to a leadership role in the modern social environment, are the children now also being wired in such a way? From early childhood, are they now more predisposed to observe female authority to extract life lessons and information that they can use later in life as adults? Including the simple idea that the female is the leader of the family.

As before, children observe their mothers and fathers in various life situations and trials, only now with the mother being the most common demonstrator. We know children have shown that they had learn from watching their parents behave. Now, with more mother's being the main demonstrators to children, the question arises. Do children benefit more from watching a mother's behavior than from watching the father's behavior?

A new study shows that a variety of brain circuits are engaged when children hear their mother's voice. Children's brains are far more engaged by their mother's voice than by any other voice, a new study from the Stanford University School of Medicine has found. Decades of research have shown that children prefer their mother's voices. In one classic study, one-day-old babies sucked harder on a pacifier when they heard the sound of their mom's voice, as opposed to any other voice.

Today, more and more women are smarter and have achieved higher levels of education than most men. And science agrees.

Lawrence Whalley, professor emeritus of the University of Aberdeen, has been researching the brain for a long time and he found that a smart woman can protect men. He said, "The thing a boy is never told he needs to do if he wants to live a longer life—but what he should do—is marry an intelligent woman. There is no better buffer than intelligence." The idea is that a smart partner never stops challenging you intellectually, which helps you keep your mental faculties keen forever.

Everyone makes mistakes and bad decisions sometimes. This makes it even more important to have someone who can get you back on track and tell you when you are wrong. Studies show that men want to have an honest partner by their side when they look for a long-term committed relationship. When a man finds an honest woman who can lead and keep him on track, he benefits greatly and lives a better life.

Many women see the glass as half-full, and Many men accuse them of naïve optimism. However, negative people are toxic and bad for our health in the long run. This is because we tend to take on the negativity of people we spend the most time with. This has been shown in various research projects, and this internalized negativity can lead to increased heart rate, impedes our digestion and lowers our concentration. In other words, it can make you sick. Sure, life is tough, but how you handle your problems can teach your man about the importance of a positive attitude.

Life can't always be a bed of roses and at some point in your relationship, you and your partner will disagree. Your response towards various problems, whether small or big, will show your man that having a positive attitude can help overcome many difficulties. Be positive and teach your man always to think positive. Encourage your man to learn from his mistakes and to never give up. It's completely normal and even inevitable. When a man has a *Love & Obey* Queen, he is comforted and remembers the idiom, "A happy wife means a happy life."

It is well-established that men and females watch the behavior of mom and try to gather useful information from their observations. A mother is the primary caregiver in most children's earliest days, weeks and months. The mother is a child's first link of any emotional bonding and attachment. A baby will learn his first emotions in relation to the mother. Children will often model their behavior as a child follows along and learns where and when to do various actions. This is the reason, that I recommend that female's reprogram and retrain badly trained older men, if the mother failed to teach them to respect and obey female authority above any other form of authority.

I expect responses to obedience commands with various men can be quite different. At any stage of the man's teaching, I usually give the obedience command to my man, using a bit of bait in the form of a positive reward. Plus reinforcing behavior in which the man is already responding correctly, at least for a certain proportion of the time.

I am not surprised that most modern men quickly adapt to female authority in the home because it reminds most of them of their mothers. Let's face it, the importance of mothers in child development is obvious. One of the first basic life skills that a child learns from a mother is to trust them and they will give you emotional security. As a *Love & Obey* Queen in a relationship, you have the onus of teaching your man about the importance of being able to trust you and to be trustworthy to you. If your man can trust you, he will be confident and emotionally secure. Be around when your man needs you and always make sure you support him and encourage him to do better. Your encouragement will show your man that your love for him is a constant, and it will make him more secure, loving and obedient.

The way you behave towards your man will have a lasting impact on your Female Led Relationship and the way he interacts with you during your life together. If you remain a kind and loving Queen towards your man, no matter how stressed or angry you are. If you respond to your man's day-to-day activities with compassion and take care of his needs you will show him the importance of being loving and cared for by a female authority figure—namely YOU! The way you speak to your man will teach him about being respectful to you and how to deal respectfully with other women as well. Men must be taught that females are the loving authority figures in their lives from birth to death and that their *Love & Obey* Queens—first the mother and then the female mate—should always be loved and obeyed.

Men can be trained to perform for women. No one can teach your man the value of hard work as much as you can! The hard work you do for your man's development and education in a Female Led Relationship is a perfect example for him. Your man may feel working hard is something that makes you tired at the end of the day. But remind him of the immense pleasure and satisfaction it gives you to see him accomplish goals for you, and the great rewards you will give him for good behavior. In his earlier days of training, your man will be most comfortable while following a set pattern in his daily life. Show your man how you can effectively manage time and commitments by following a routine. Teach your man the importance of discipline and make sure you also follow some basic routines in your daily life and make him obey your rules in the relationship.

It is common for men to break the rules of a Female Led Relationship and go against you in order to 'test' your real authority. Only that way do they understand what behavior is appropriate and what is not. When your man talks back to you, it may seem manly and asexy at first, but when your man shouts out "No!"every time you tell him to do something, it will eventually get on your nerves. If not handled properly, backtalk from your man can lead to arguments and eventually breakups. So what do you do?

1. If your man talks back but follows your instructions, then ignore it. Ignoring backtalk may be okay if the behavior is not threatening or destructive.

2. If the man follows instructions, even though he talks back, appreciate that they did what you asked, even if they didn't want to. But when he is calm, explain that it is okay to be angry sometimes, but never okay to speak to you disrespectfully.

3. But if the man's response is threatening, then you need to pay attention to what they say and handle it carefully. Any man who has nothing better to do then threaten a woman has some serious issues. He is a bully, on a power trip, and a loser. Leave him before he does exactly what he keeps threatening to do. You do not need to fear the man that you are in a relationship with or dating. What kind of fun is there in seeing someone who you have to fear? Get out of the relationship before you get hurt or worse. Just get out!

4. Do not respond impulsively. Let the man calm down and then address what he said. Tell him calmly about what behavior is acceptable and what is not.

5. Set limits and make them aware of the consequences. Do not threaten, just state plain facts that if they talk back, they won't get to watch their favorite movie, eat food they like or have sex with you.

6. Set expectations for his behavior, tell him that if he is rude or disrespectful, he will be denied rewards and only receive punishment and what fun is that?

There is one interesting observational nuance that I have noticed in Female Led Relationships, namely that the men who were a little bit older seemed to be easier to train and more open to *Love & Obey* Queenship, presumably based on the fact that after a lifetime of experiencing women, and being more defiant and abusive when they are younger, they have learned that eventually you must give in to female authority or be a lonely old man.

CHAPTER 14

Note: *This last instructional Chapter is for the Queen to read even more than you. It summarizes for the Queen what is needed for the perfect Female Led Relationship. It is good for you to read it as well, since as I mentioned earlier, you both want to cooperate in the learning and training process so you can get your FLR working flawlessly in no time at all.*

Men can be stubborn. Here are some great strategies for teaching a stubborn man. Training a stubborn man can be frustrating—I've worked with dozens of men who feel like they're on the losing end of a battle of wills with their female companions. I've also had several difficult-to-train men of my own over the years. When bad habits refuse to budge, women can wind up feeling frustrated, exhausted and defeated.

If you're struggling to train your man, don't give up! There's hope for even the most challenging men. The solution may be as simple as changing your approach to teaching.

When a man will not listen to or follow your commands, it's not typically because he is hardheaded or untrainable. The problem is often that old-fashioned male behavior that comes naturally to many men, simply doesn't conform to the new FLR standards of good manners. And changing roles for men and women in our future female led society, so it can take some time and effort to reprogram your man.

This doesn't necessarily mean a complete revision of your *Love & Obey* training program with every new man. However, for some men, even the smallest shift in the teaching process can make a big difference in your success.

Love and Obey Strategies for Stubborn Men.

A few simple tweaks can make all the difference if your man's behavior is challenging. Here are seven of my favorite strategies for stubborn men:

Go slowly. Start by working with your man on favorite or familiar behaviors. Create a positive association with teaching by rewarding him for even minor successes. Once your man understands that his training is a good and pleasurable thing for him, he will change. Take tiny steps. Change only one variable at a time. Once your man has mastered one behavior, you want him to do add another small improvement to your list. Take your time, and if teaching him becomes too hard, your man is likely to give up (and so are you).

Control the environment. During your teaching sessions, take precautions to keep your man focused. Choose a distraction-free area like your kitchen or living room. Put away any distractions or items that he may be tempted to pay attention to, like the television. Even a well-trained man can be tempted by an NFL football game or the Victoria Secret Swimsuit Special.

Be consistent. Do not ask for the same behavior in different ways or reward him in ways for various behaviors. Your man may seem stubborn when he's really just confused about what you want. Use consistent cues or commands for what you want and keep it simple. Offer him consistent rewards, and it is more likely that your man will do what he's asked to do. So, if you are trying to teach your man to do the dishes for you, make sure you don't allow him to skip it when you don't mind doing the dishes. Get him trained to do the dishes, and after he has been trained, you can have some flexibility.

Avoid punishment. Punishment increases anxiety and undermines your man's trust in you. In the long-term, punishment can lead to a higher risk of aggression. That's why I strongly push for reward-based training. Reward tactics that focus on giving the man things he desires with rewards, like movies, shows, sporting events and of course the big one—SEX—when he responds to a command in the desired manner. And rather than punishing him for unwanted behavior, redirect him to a more acceptable behavior, and then show him a good time in the bedroom.

Choose the right rewards. Make sure that your teaching is relevant by making certain that the behavior you desire is highly rewarding for your man. If rewards are infrequent or boring to your man, his response is likely to be bad. Increasing the value and frequency of your rewards can often dramatically improve your man's response—and his behavior. Different men value different things; figure out what your man loves most and offer that in return for good behavior. Rewards can include watching favorite shows and movies, going to special sporting or cultural events, like concerts or buying certain electronic devices or other male products for him. And, of course, the number one reward all men want: Sexual rewards! **Your golden training rule should be: Control your sex with you man and give it to**

him only when he behaves the way you want! If he misbehaves deny, deny, deny him!

Make teaching a habit. Don't think about teaching as a once-a-day event—make it part of your daily routine. To reinforce wanted behavior, engage your man in short teaching sessions throughout the day. This can be as simple as asking your man for a specific desired behavior, such as a making you a cup of tea, and rewarding his success with something favorable to him.

As I have discussed before, there is no one individual who influences the development of a child more than the mother. Every aspect of a child's progression through life, beginning with their genetic makeup, is greatly influenced, if not completely determined, by the mother in the child's life. The mother creates the climate which the child will grow up in. Whether that is in regard to family dynamics, intellectual stimulation, or social development. One way mother's dictate the development of a child is through discipline. The methods and means of disciplining a child can impact their life socially, behaviorally and even intellectually.

Many women who have men who do not behave properly, and do not serve their needs as they desire, ask me whether a man can be too old to teach him what needs to be done to make you happy. I tell them that male behavior modification is certainly something that should be done in all men as early as possible. I wish all mothers started training their male children from infancy to love and obey women. I wish that all mother's would teach their boys that at every level of the child's development that he should be trained to behave in a way that makes the *Love & Obey* Queen happy—first the mother leader and then later the female partner. Thankfully, many mothers do teachthat obedience is good behavior and disobedience of the female is bad. Our job as adult females would be much easier when it comes to training men that we meet to behave as we desire. At least they would already be trained to love, obey and serve women when they choose to enter a relationship.

I believe there is no "time that is too late" to modify a man's behavior but the earlier females can begin training them to love, honor, obey and serve the better. However, it is always time to do this is when the *Love & Obey* Queen has come to the conclusion that their man's behavior is not pleasing to her and that he is merely too disruptive, and needs to change the way he acts.

Classical conditioning theory is when we learn a new behavior by the process of association. In simple terms, two stimuli are linked together to produce a new learned response in a person. Together with operant conditioning, classical conditioning became the foundation of behaviorism, a school that was dominant in the mid-20th century and is still an important influence on the practice of and the study of human behavior. Classical conditioning is a basic learning process, and its neural substrates are now beginning to be understood.

Classical conditioning occurs when a conditioned stimulus is paired with an unconditioned stimulus. Usually, the conditioned stimulus is a neutral stimulus, such as the sound of you saying "Attaboy," the unconditioned stimulus is biologically potent "a sexual experience" and the unconditioned response to the unconditioned stimulus is an unlearned reflex response "an erection." After pairing is repeated and some learning may occur after only one pairing, the man can exhibit a conditioned response to the conditioned stimulus when it is presented alone.

This method may effectively keep a child "in line," but they could be harmful in the long-term. One such example of this damaging discipline is corporal punishment and a Female Domination BDSM/FEMDOM approach to a Female Led Relationship. The Female Domination BDSM/FEMDOM approach naturally creates a disconnect between the dominatrix and the man. It is a relationship of power exercised by the female over the man, with little mutual understanding or discussion. A relationship run in this style can be effective in some ways and for some time, but it comes with many dangers for the man's future as many men experience nothing but a lack of understanding of their needs. Some Female Led BDSM/FEMDOM relationships take this approach to a new level. It encourages strong discipline in the face of any sort of disobedience. It takes the stance that women have dominion over their men, and thus, should exercise absolute power over them.

The dominatrix encourages regular use of corporal punishment for any offense. This regular use of violence is not only emotionally and physically traumatizing and confusing for the man, it can also result in a perverse form of classical conditioning. As the man is regularly beaten for wrongdoings, they begin to associate the implement of violence as a form of female affection. The men often associate the voice of their dominatrix with their only love, and this abuse and physical and psychological suffering somehow becomes pleasurable for them in a disturbing way. Such a strong negative relationship between female and male results in a very unhealthy relationships for the man (and even the woman) in the future with peers, authority figures, and eventually the world.

So, I must stress that classical and operant conditioning can prove to be harmful as well. Both are powerful ways to alter human behavior and dangers do not only lie in extreme BDSM/FEMDOM approaches to relationships, such as the one described above. But with other milder examples of female disciplinary lifestyles that can also be harmful to future relationships of a man socially. If classical conditioning is used to create a BDSM/FEMDOM slave, or Skinner's disciplinary practices are used with a female's mate that are not consistent with love and compassion, the man can develop bad behaviors that will alter his entire adult life.

Operant conditioning and classical conditioning have both shown that a reward for good behavior and punishment for bad behavior are an effective means of social development and training. However, it is also clear that if discouragement of certain positive behaviors like love, compassion, thoughtfulness, tenderness and kindness are not firmly used in training in a consistent and meaningful way, then the man will only learn to seek "BDSM/FEMDOM" behavior in hopes of hitting an emotional relationship with a woman again. This type of behavior can evolve into a depraved adulthood. In order to prevent this for any man, a *Love & Obey* Queen must be consistently loving in their rewards of men. A mixture of reward and punishment are beneficial as long as they remain constantly positive and loving toward the man over the long-term.

Considering each of the four modes of behavioral conditioning—positive reinforcement, negative reinforcement, positive punishment, and negative punishment —not every method alters undesirable behavior in men equally. Research has shown that negative reinforcement used to reduce certain behaviors may unintentionally exasperate men. I believe in practicing positive discipline; positive reinforcement has prolific effects on a man's behavior. I believe that female attention, time, and verbal encouragement are perhaps the most effective tools in enhancing desirable behaviors; and indeed, men require the acceptance and emotional support of their *Love & Obey* Queen in order to develop properly in cognitive, social and emotional domains.

I know from experience that if the man spends more time behaving desirably, he or she will, consequently, spend less time behaving undesirably. Eventually, all desired behaviors have been positively reinforced so frequently that they significantly outnumber undesired behaviors and constitute the majority of the man's energy and attentional investment, hopefully streamlining the positive outcomes available to the man over the course of the relationship. Basically, the man becomes focused on behaving in a way that is constantly making his Queen happy, and therefore, bringing him positive reinforcement and the rewards that he desires, like sexually pleasuring the female. Naturally, positive reinforcement sustains positive development with consistency, an aspect of a loving Female Led Relationship that is particularly important to maintain. So, when a man does what you desire, when he behaves in a manner that is pleasing to you, you must reward him appropriately to the action. Fix him a special meal, or give him sex as a reward. Let him make love to you. Buy him the new model of iPhone that he wants. Let him go to a sporting event. Allow him to orgasm, etc.

From personal experience, I always ensure that I make my man follow consistent rules, such as his consistent bedtime (every night I tell my man that is time for him to go to bed and if he has been respectful in regard to my wishes and desires all day, he knows I will probably allow him to make love to me). In this way, I teach him that there are predictable features in our relationship and that his behavior will evoke consistent results of "positive rewards" aligned with his actions and behavior. For example, he knows that calling me "Queen" will produce a positive response in me, and if he continues to act respectfully towards me, he will experience a positive emotional reinforcement and reward for his behavior. Interestingly, some women teach their men in a more permissive style, allowing them ambiguous bedtimes and little instruction regarding how they should address the woman. In consequence, the man's behavior often proves problematic for the Queen since the man does not know how to behave consistently. As such, the responsibility for establishing correct man behavior (however you define it) will be her job. Every man's successful training is contingent on consistent, positive reinforcement resulting from a loving authoritative female.

With every man who does not behave in a manner that is desirable for the *Love & Obey* Queen, successfully teaching him how to love, obey and serve you on his own really depends upon you sticking to your guns. And giving the man a consistent message that, while you still **love** him, he must follow the rules of how he is to behave, and that he really has no choice in the matter. This is usually done by denying the man any sexual rewards, and letting him get more and more frustrated until he finally starts to behave as you have instructed him on his own. Praising him with audio or verbal cues at fixed intervals to reassure him that he will be rewarded when his behavior pleases you and that as soon as he changes his behavior his reward will be coming, despite his moodiness and pouting, he will survive and be happy once he becomes obedient. That is why it is so important to implement the rules of what you like and what you don't like in behavior from the very earliest time in your relationship as possible. Make sure that he has a regular, appropriate schedule and regular behavior routines to follow that please you.

With a slightly older man, who has not been trained and perhaps you just met, it is never too late to learn, informing him of your list of expectations for his behavior. Posting them on the bedroom door can be a very effective means of making sure that he gets the message.

If you want to enter this bedroom and be rewarded, you will behave in a manner that is pleasing and that makes me as your *Love & Obey* Queen happy. The message on the door essentially turns the entire bedroom into a powerful reminder that his positive rewards will come with positive behavior. Most women do this somewhat unconsciously and most men often comment that they don't get as much sex as they used to from their woman as they did when they were dating you. Men just don't get it and the need to learn! When men are in the dating phase of their relationship they behave in a manner that is pleasing to you as the female who they are courting most of the time, or eventually you will stop dating. Men are trying to win the affection of the female, and the females are consistently in a good mood because he is behaving in a pleasing way to you. So, you reward him with sex on a regular basis because he is making you happy. In a long-term relationship, the man is often allowed to get lazier and lazier and less attentive to what you want and desire to make you happy. He becomes more thoughtless and less considerate of your wants and needs. Naturally, you just don't feel like rewarding him with sex at the end of a day when he has done nothing to make you happy. I don't see why men simply can't see the simple picture. Love, obey and do as your woman desires and behave in a manner that will make her happy and please her and you will have two times, three times and even four times more sex than you do now. Perhaps you will be so happy you will want to have sex with him every day and probably even more than most older men can even handle. The men should stop their complaining about how once you get married, you will rarely have sex and realize that if they behaved properly, they would be rewarded consistently with sex! While cutting a man off at the bedroom door from pleasure can generate a lot of anxiety with the man and make him wonder if his woman has abandoned him, or if he is going to be punished forever because he is married, it is important to lay down the law. Behave properly and as I desire and you will be rewarded with more love (sex) than you ever imagined possible. Men do not cheat in Female Led Relationships because they are well trained and obedient. The reason why men cheat in traditional relationships is because women do not demand proper behavior from them. Here are the four simple steps that occur on the path to male infidelity:

- ❖ **STEP ONE:** The woman is not happy with the man's behavior.

- ❖ **STEP TWO:** She cuts him off from sex. Once this happens, his anxiety can become so strong the man begins to get ideas.

- ❖ **STEP THREE:** He goes out to find another female who will have sex with him. Ironically, he rewards the new female properly, showering her with attention and behaving properly to win her affection. The way he would be treating you in an FLR.

- ❖ **STEP FOUR:** The other woman gives him sex because he is behaving properly and pleasing her.

Ladies, do yourself and your man a favor, demand proper behavior. Lead the relationship and make your man behave in a way that pleases you and then reward him with sex consistently for his consistently good behavior. This consistent good behavior and positive reward experience is the ultimate goal of teaching him to love and obey you and it is the end goal of the Female Led Relationship. This is why they say "Happy wife, Happy life!" It's really simple, if you think about it. "If mama is happy, everybody's happy!"

When one tries to change the behavior patterns in an older man, enlisting his understanding of this formula for success and his active cooperation is critical to achieving success. This is done by explaining to him the behavior that makes you happy and then implementing his reward system, with the man earning rewards for doing behavior that pleases you on his own.

You can even make up a list of behavior that bothers you and how you want him to change, list on the chart the behavior that will make you happy and even listing the reward he will receive for performing these behaviors can be used as an incentive to get him to cooperate with the process.

For example, if good hygiene pleases you, on any given day, if you want a man to improve his grooming and he showers, shaves, puts on cologne, brushes his teeth and styles his hair the way you like, entirely on his own, compliment him with an "Attaboy" immediately and make love to him like you did when you were dating. If he massages your feet, entirely on his own, do it again; if he brings you a cup of tea and a snack on his own, do it again; but if he spends the day unwashed, unshaven, smelling like an alley cat, bad breath and has no hair style, GIVE HIM NOTHING.

If after a good desirable behavior, the man receives a predetermined reward, it doesn't have to be sex, but generally that always works. It's your greatest power over him, whether you want to accept that fact, or not. After bad undesirable behavior, the man receives a NOTHING. Eventually he will learn to LOVE AND OBEY.

Setting goals for him can be overwhelming. It is often that this "overwhelming" comes in the form of overzealous goal setting. The most important step to learning how to be a *Love & Obey* Queen is to attain the fine balance of leadership; awareness, priorities, effort and time. Here are some techniques that work for some women, when teaching their man to behave properly:

1. **HAVE SPECIFIC GOALS FOR HIM.** Set little goals. This is the best way to get men moving toward big goals. Meeting a goal gives a man an incredible surge of energy. It is important to teach men that every goal you set is worth attaining. Listen to what your man likes and wants in his life, and then steer him gently towards what you want which corresponds in some way to what he likes. Give your man realistic goals that he can actually accomplish. Make sure to take baby steps with him at first. One new behavior a day, such as picking up after himself, sitting down on the toilet seat when he pees, or any behavior—like better grooming—that you desire. Then set an amount of time of when you want it completed and let him know. Pick one goal at a time if necessary. You know your man best. Crafting a vision board or making a list of the "dream behaviors" that you know he can live up to and picking the ones that are in his area of interest are essential. For example, if he is a handy guy, then select tasks around the house that you want fixed. When he spends his time fixing them, reward him.

2. **GIVE HIM THE RIGHT TOOLS.** You can make a good behavior kit for your man. This could be a calendar, timer, a marker or a log of some sort to maintain the good behaviors that you set and when he achieves them, and a note on how he was rewarded.

3. **PLAN THE WORK IT TAKES**. Every new good behavior takes a different amount of time and energy to achieve. It is important to ensure the man thinks through the steps it will take to achieve the behavior that you want from him.

4. **FOCUS ON THE TIME**. Something that many men lack is an awareness of time. Make sure you mark the calendar or teach them to keep their log for everything they need to achieve to keep you happy and when they achieve it. This is a great way to educate them about time awareness, taking breaks, moderation and reaching your goal of good behavior. Remember, consistently good behavior earns consistent rewards from the *Love & Obey* Queen.

Beware of counter conditioning. Behavioral conditioning does not always involve the acquisition of any new good behavior, but can teach the man to respond in old ways, if you reward him without any new and good behavior, so keep setting goals and taking his behavior to new heights. There is no limit to how perfectly your man can be trained to behave the way you desire. A critical problem with rewarding a man with sex, when he has done nothing to deserve it, is that he will think that he is entitled to a reward even if he acts in his same old, unpleasing way with you. It is important to keep daily baby steps moving forward. With each new step, another reward. With each old bad behavior rising up—NOTHING!

Keep the reward appropriate and let him learn that the bigger his behavioral improvements, the bigger his rewards. Make sure you assign an "associative strength" for the behavior to the reward. Every time he combs his hair doesn't mean he deserves to mount you. Before you begin behavioral conditioning, figure out an associative reward for each new behavior that you want to teach your man. The bigger the behavior that you want to teach him, the more you will gradually increase the associative strength of the reward he receives. This increase is determined by the nature of the behavior that you desire. The amount of learning that is required of him, and the amount of time and effort it takes for him to learn the new desired behavior will determine his reward. If he combs his hair the way you like, perhaps he deserves an "Attaboy" and a kiss on the cheek! If the behavioral change is large, then the associative strength of the reward takes a big step up. As you teach him new behaviors, and his experience of what you want him accumulates in his mind, the reward becomes more predictable. And the increase in associative strength of each reward can be smaller. Finally, the difference between the associative strength of a minor behavioral change and the corresponding reward, and the maximum strength reward for a major change will become established in his mind. That is, he will fully be able to predict the associative strength of the reward with his experience, and once he knows all the behavior and the corresponding reward he will receive, his conditioning will be complete. At that point he will behave as you like on his own.

Once he really steps up and behaves like a total gentleman, and rewards you with his total obedience and a lifestyle worthy of a great Queen, you need to make sure that you also step up and let him make love to you. Once you achieve the adoring gentleman who worships you and you become the undisputed Queen of the house, you will be living in a loving Female Led Relationship. You will experience bliss of a honeymoon that lasts forever. So, go enjoy a Female Led Relationship and all its passion and pleasure.

CHAPTER 15

> "A man must obey his Love & Obey Queen in everything she commands. A man must try to please her all the time, not just when she is watching him. A man must serve her sincerely because of his love and respect for her."
>
> — Marisa Rudder

The future is female and hopefully one day this book will no longer be needed as future generations of women are brought up as the dominant leaders of society and men are taught that their purpose in life is to love, obey and serve women. Today, we can see lifestyles and gender roles are changing and Queens are rising in business, art, education, entertainment, politics, sports and lifestyles. So, congratulations, you are an important part of this change because you have chosen to live a female led lifestyle, right now, today! You are now a leader in the change to a female led world. Every man and women who is part of the *Love & Obey* movement are making a difference. A large amount of change is required, and we must reprogram and reinforce female superiority.

Respect for female authority over men is necessary to achieve a successful and fully functioning FLR. I know that even in relationships with an enthusiastic and accepting man, who truly desires to enter into a loving Female Led Relationship, it is not always an easy road. As you have read in this book, there are many obstacles to overcome when creating your own Female Led Relationship. You even have to figure out which style will work best for you. I have given you guidelines and ideas that you can use to set up your FLR, but it depends on what kind of dominant woman and obedient man you are, and what you both desire in the relationship. Whether you both want a mild or extreme Female Led Relationship, many women and most men must be retrained and reprogrammed from the patriarchal male-dominated upbringing in which most of us grew up with and is still dominant in most societies around the world.

In my marriage, my husband is an attractive, intelligent, and aggressive man when dealing with other men in the outside world, and he is not alone in FLR. But he bows before me as his Queen. Many successful and strong men are smart enough to know that females are naturally superior and they freely choose to kneel before their Queen or Goddess. But even if your man is an alpha male, even if he is a submissive beta male or somewhere in between, the end result is the same. Global leadership must be transferred by men to women, so we can experience the natural wonder of loving female authority ruling over our relationships, cities, states, nations and eventually the world. *Real Men Worship Women* and are happy to *Love & Obey*. So, congratulations, good luck and be proud on living a female led lifestyle—this is the future.

www.ingramcontent.com/pod-product-compliance
Lightning Source LLC
Chambersburg PA
CBHW021237090426
42740CB00006B/574